W9-BGM-259

RAJON RONDO: SUPERSTAR!

(The Green Years)

Third Edition

William Russo

Copyright 2012 by William Russo
All rights reserved. No part of this book may be reproduced or transmitted in any form or by any means, electronic or mechanical, including photocopying, recording, or by information storage and retrieval systems without the permission in writing from the copyright owner.

LONG TIME AGO BOOKS
Third Edition

Humorist and Boston Celtics fan William Russo puts together this collection of more than 50 funny and poignant essays on Rajon Rondo, presenting him during several of his remarkable seasons in Boston—and through the heart-breaking 2012 playoffs.

Not always flattering to Rajon, but always whimsical, these portraits of the Boston Celtics point guard are incisive and may touch a nerve with fans.

If—like King Arthur--Rondo pulled the sword from the stone, then he had to be recognized as the true leader of the Celtics. These tales document the legend and myth of Rajon Rondo.

With wit and literary allusion, Russo puts Rondo directly into the center of American sports myth, predicting that the Boston Celtics PG may be looking at a future that resembles Norse and Viking war tales. Not exactly a biography, the stories recount the impact and affection Rondo's fans have for him.

Some of these essays appeared on MTR Media.com, the Spoof, and on Boston.com. Other pieces also were featured in sports collections by the author.

RAJON RONDO: SUPERSTAR (The Green Years)

TABLE OF CONTENTS

PART THREE
2012 POST SEASON

Bombs Away as Rajon Rondo Turns into a Super Nova

Valentine and Rondo: Together in Our Bad Dreams

Rondo Faces the Music: Off Key Again

Rondo Sings "Positively 4th Estate" to Boston Media

Rondo and Teddy: Boston Has Seen It All Before…

Rondo Names That Tune in Two Notes

Augurs Tell the Tale of Pierce and Rondo

Mitt Romney is a Celtic

Rondo Explodes for a Slam Dunk

Rondo Overexposed by Blow Up

Every Game with the Celtics is an Old Timers Game

No Horsing Around: Paul Pierce is on Bronco Garnett

Assist Machine Rajon Rondo Breaks Down the Game

Boston Celtics at the O.K. Corral

Scrooge and Rondo Share the Ball

Green Sneakers or Green Eggs: The Yoke is on the Celtics

Boston Mayor Malaprop Mouths Off at the Celtics

Celtics Have a Dickens of a Run

Rondo Becomes the Real Deal: a Superstar!

AND, AT LAST--
Celtics Big Three: The Next Generation

INTRODUCTION

The Three Musketeers Were Truly a Fearsome Foursome

So often the city of Boston and its media have tried to find the right nickname for Kevin Garnett, Paul Pierce, and Ray Allen. They were the second coming, and thus dubbed The Big Three.

What happened after their championship run was that a young pup of a point guard seemed appended to their threesome. Some saw him as an afterthought; others thought he deserved to join the special bond. A few cynics called him out for riding on the coattails of the superstars of the Celtics.

What many failed to recall was that the original Three Musketeers were actually four men.

In the original tale, young D'Artagnon travels to Paris, much like young Rondo traveled to Boston. Each of the Big Three, like the Musketeers, challenge the young man to play at the highest level. The original Musketeers were Athos, Aramis, and Porthos, while the modern Musketeers are Ray, Paul, and Kevin.

In the recent documentary on the Celtics 2011 season, entitled "The Association," Rondo reveals that his own challenge from the intimidating Garnett resulted in a fight in the locker-room during the young guard's first season.

Kevin Garnett's powerful influence is a point of approval. After their scuffle, Rondo was accepted into the special club. He was deemed the crown prince to the Big Three. They would insure his success and teach him how to be a winner.

From his early season with the new Big Three, Rondo managed to hold his own and then become a force with the Big Three. Few people remember that there were Four Musketeers, not three. The man outside the Three Musketeers was D'Artagnon, their leader and spiritual force.

The Three Musketeers could do any feat of derring-do, but it was D'Artagnon who directed their successful actions.

So it is with the Celtics. Rajon Rondo has become so entwined with the legendary status of the Big Three that he shall inevitably be part of them as D'Artagnon was the Fourth Musketeer.

PART ONE
2010-2011 Season

A Trek From the Outer Limits to the Rajon Rondo Zone

You are now entering the Rajon Rondo Zone.

There is nothing wrong with your cable television. Do not attempt to adjust the point guard. He is controlling transmission.

If Rondo wishes to make the crowds sound louder, he will bring up the volume. If he wishes to make a soft pass, he will tune down the Big 3 to a whisper. He will control the offense. He will control the defense.

Rondo can roll the images you see. He can make your heart flutter. He can change the focus of the game to a soft blur or sharpen it to crystal clarity.

For the entire 48 minutes, sit in quiet desperation, and Rondo will control all that you see and hear.

The Boston Celtics want to repeat:

There is nothing wrong with your cable television reception. You are about to participate in a great adventure. You are about to experience the awe and mystery which reaches from the inner mind of Rajon Rondo to... the NBA Finals.

The NBA Finals.

The final frontier where no team has gone 18 times and won. These are the adventures of the Boston Celtics whose mission is to explore combinations off the bench, to seek out life on planet Rondo, and to boldly go where no point guard has gone before…

There is another dimension to the Boston Celtics, a fifth dimension, beyond that which is known to mortal NBA teams.

For a team to reach 18 banners, you must enter a dimension beyond Twitterverse, outside the realm of social networks, into a dimension as vast and as timeless as infinity.

Yes, the Celtics want Rondo to take them to that odd field, between light and shadow, between science of angles and three-point shots.

For Rondo, victory lies between the pit of his defensive lapses and the summit of his knowledge.

This is the dimension of competitive imagination. It is an area that Boston Celtics call The Rondo Conundrum.

Fans are traveling through another dimension after the trade of Perk and Nate, not only of sight and sound, but of mind's fury from a point guard scorned.

Will it be a journey into a wondrous land whose boundaries are that of Los Angeles or of Chicago?

That's the signpost up ahead: Your next stop: The Playoffs.

You unlock this door to the playoffs with the key player called Rondo.

Beyond the door is another dimension, a dimension of sound, a dimension of sight, a dimension of mind.

You are moving into a playoff series of both alley-oops and peculiar passes, of palpitating moments and of streaks of temperament.

You have just crossed over into the Rondo Zone.

(Special thanks to Rod Serling, Gene Roddenberry, and Robert Bloch.)

Rajon Rondo's Roll and Bounce

Rajon Rondo does not sweat.

This Boston Celtic point guard will run up and down the court for ten minutes, do fancy footwork, charge through the trees, and hit the target. He exerts tons of energy and power, but looks serene.

Rajon may sit on the bench for a rest now and then, but once stuck between a sopping Kendrick Perkins, or soaking Kevin Garnett, Rondo is pristine and dry.

Unlike other teammates who use a dozen towels to dry off, Rondo merely uses towels as decorative and fashionable statements of his rumored status as the best-dressed Celtic off the court, and as the best roller-blade skater in the NBA.

Why then does sweat-free Rondo wear an upside down sweatband on his head?

Many years ago Red Auerbach once saw another Celtic whom he noted did not sweat. This he attributed to being "in perfect shape." The sweat-free player was a legend among legends: John Havlicek.

His nickname was Hondo.

So, here we are, with perspiration history repeating itself in Boston: Rondo Meet Hondo.

As far as known, Hondo did not roller dance, or at least admit to it. Rondo's roller-blade prowess may be one of the secrets of his ability to keep the drips to a minimum.

Baptized With The Name Game

If point guard Rajon Rondo's name strikes you as familiar, or special, or rarefied, you may be more than a little correct.

Though Rajon is Latvian for "District", the word "Rondo" has growing resonance in NBA terminology. The name rondo has its roots in poetry and music, which also resembles Rajon Rondo's ball movements and body language.

A rondo is a motif of classical music, like the repeated action of an alley-oop between the point guard and Kevin Garnett, seen in its spectacular form nearly every game.

In music rondo refers to fast and vivacious style, like the ultimate up-tempo player himself.

A classical rondo featured a popular or folk character. Today in Boston, Rajon Rondo surely has managed to blend perfectly his folk hero role among three future Hall of Fame players who'd dominate other point guards, but play at his beck and call.

Those of a certain age from the 1960s will also recall that Rondo was a blended hybrid, dark-skinned grape that came to be the essence of in the making of a rich ruby-red wine.

Its ability to mature early gave it high resistance to winter frost and dangerous mildew. Like the essence of the Rondo wine, our Celtic tends toward yielding colorful play and has a panache that is unmistakable.

A decade later Rondo was a popular citrus soft drink from the 1970s whose formula was "blended from fine essences", and "lightly carbonated," sort of like the Celtic version of Rondo.

That pop drink, the Rondo, became known as "The Thirst Crusher," and inspired people to crush empty cans with creative authority in their commercials. Boston's Rondo crushes every opposing team and has satisfied the thirst for another Celtics championship.

Rondo Days is an annual weekend festival held in mid-July in Saint Paul, Minnesota, that commemorates the Rondo neighborhood of Africa, and in Boston we now enjoy a season full of Rondo days and nights, game time festivals in which we can never be sure what new flashes of brilliance we will see.

Another variation of Rondo is the French spelling as "Rondeau." This is a poem of 13 lines in 3 stanzas. Nothing is lost in translation, because a Celtic Rondo is sort of like a point guard among a team of 12 players and 3 superstars.

In Medieval times, a troubadour went around singing the classic Rondo. Today in Boston Celtic fans are singing the praises of the neo-classic Rondo.

Could there be a name more appropriate for the Celtics than Rondo, their youngest star who turned 23 recently?

Cooking Up a Storm With Shannon Allen on TV!

What's the best way to wheedle an interview with insights?

Take the subject to dinner. And, beautiful, charming, and disarming Shannon Allen, wife of Celtics star Ray, did just that on her spicy new cooking show on Boston's cable sports network, taped at the Seaport Hotel complex.

Each week, Shannon will cook up a storm and serve it to the athlete of choice. On the menu in future shows will be Wes Welker, Glen Davis, and Kevin Youkilis, and of course, Ray Allen.

In mid-February as the show's guest, Rajon Rondo looked bemused at the camera during the cooking sequence when Shannon asked him to do a modicum of labor, like beating up cornflakes for the crispy chicken.

The Celtics point guard is obviously not used to taking orders, but prefers giving them. And, that includes general of the troop on the basketball court and at work in the kitchen. He confessed he did all the cooking at home growing up and once considered going to culinary school.

It appears Rajon (and he informs everyone how to pronounce his name correctly on this show) may be the general in his own culinary den. He does much of his own healthy meal preparing at home both in season and off, especially since he wants his daughter to eat healthy.

Rondo takes an opportunity to point out how little body fat he has (lowest in the league he boasts proudly). The spitfire guard attributed the condition to youth, not yet overly worried about his dietary intake like the oldsters on the team who surround him. Of course, his natural tenacity of competition came across in every contest with his teammates.

Taped before the infamous trades by the Celtics at the end of February, Rajon noted how great the camaraderie has been with this team, especially off the court. He confessed they acted like brothers, even to the point of fighting a bit. It makes the loss since the taping more palpable.

If Rajon loves cornbread, how can there be any surprise? Eating cornbread became a superstitious ritual during the Celtics run for the championship when players ate together during the playoffs in 2008. Lucky for Rondo, former Celtics player and current radio analyst Cedric Maxwell has already stolen the nickname "Cornbread."

Only one player's name (other than Ray) crossed Rondo's lips. Perhaps he put the curse of the "unfried chicken" meal on Kendrick Perkins.

Though Rondo observed he was a big eater, only Perkins could wolf down four pizzas at a meal, reported his friend. The scene has turned bittersweet with Perk now half across the country and in another division.

The twosome often compared to Steinbeck's Lenny and George may have had their last Celtic meal together. Small George, the brains of the two in *Of Mice and Men,* often controlled physically imposing Lennie and his fierce anger.

How often Rondo pushed Perk away from angry confrontations, saving him plenty of technical fouls. Now the Lenny figure will move on to Oklahoma City where his thunderous attitude will find no leash to help him stay out of on-court trouble.

But, we still have Rajon. He finally admits he is the hot sauce guy on the Celtics. And, he knows he is "fortunate" to be on a team that "gets along very well," explaining the recent turmoil over the trade of Perkins.

Those fans that are lucky enough can find the "Pre-Game Meal" show, with Shannon Allen, available on Comcast stations.

Rajon Rondo gives us plenty to chew on.

Feat for Feet: A Race Among Rondo, Welker, Crawford & Ellsbury?

Forget the Boston Marathon. What about the 40-yard dash?

Boston needs to have a new race. The opportunity is rare, and the competition is fierce.

American cities rarely produce great teams in each major sport at the same time. Only Boston seems to have a footrace of epic proportions unfolding in their professional athletic midst. This year Boston has teams in their three major sports that have all-star athletes who are the speediest at their game, 20-something stars that show flashes of brilliance in each game they play.

Blessed already with an outfielder whose speed is well documented, the Boston Red Sox enjoyed the torrid pace of Jacoby Ellsbury, tracking down balls in center field (where he shall return in 2011), and gloated over the young runner who stole home against the Yankees in a game.

Now, Ellsbury finds himself aside Carl Crawford, arguably the fastest man in all baseball. Crawford's base stealing is a modern sideshow. Together with Ellsbury, they may steal every catcher blind this upcoming season, and all in the same game in the same city, at the same time.

Merely the tip of the Boston running glut, speedy players dominate the sports scene in football and basketball too.

At TD Garden with the Boston Celtics, Rajon Rondo has shown flashes that befit a hare among tortoises.

At Gillette Stadium for the New England Patriots, another alliterative runner has come back from knee troubles to show his speed and acumen for another season. Wes Welker shows flashes of speed while dragging behemoth tackles with him.

What other city has had such speedy players all in different sports all at the same time?

How fast are these athletes? Rumors abound when it comes to the 40-yard dash.

Carl Crawford claims to have done it in 4.27 seconds.

Jacoby Ellsbury's fastest speed has been reported to be 4.28 seconds.

Rajon Rondo has boasted that he has done it in 4.35 seconds.

And, Wes Welker seems to have lumbered across the finish line in 4.5 seconds.

Let the debate begin on who deserves the title of the fleet-footed Mercury of Boston.

Rondo and Welker seldom run in a straight line, and their pivots while maintaining speed is impressive. All these stars, at the peaks of their careers, may never be faster. How on earth can we test them and settle the debate? If you cannot get four athletes in such close proximity to race to settle the score, the feat will never be flatly settled anywhere.

Rondo has not been shy about challenging various athletes to a race. The others are equally competitive. Boston needs some kind charity to step forward and to arrange the race of the 21st Century.

Who'd win? Inquiring minds may number in the millions. The race would likely be settled by a hundredth of a second.

Kevin Garnett's Movie Parallels: Boston Celtics Plot Thickens

This week Kevin Garnett compared himself and fellow Boston Celtics to characters in the classic caper film, *Ocean's 11*. No, no, not the one with the original Rat Pack, but the latest with George Clooney, Brad Pitt, Matt Damon, *etc*. KG immediately identified himself as the old expert (played by Carl Reiner).

In fact, there are many old movies KG might find himself emulating. Here are a few:

The Wild Bunch
A group of aging basketball players win a championship. Many fans believe the old players (Garnett, Pierce, Allen, Shaq) simply can no longer keep up. The times are changing, technology advancing, and their style of life is getting left behind in the dust that they spent so long galloping through. They consider abandoning their careers for the simpler life of retirement, but sign on for one more big season. At this time the new Big Three (LeBron James and gang) is always on their tracks, worse than bounty hunters.

The Magnificent Seven
Seven men (Garnett, Allen, Pierce, Rondo, West, Shaq, Big Baby) are picked to guard Boston from Miami Banditos (Lebron James, Dwayne Wade, Chris Bosh) that come every now and then to take whatever players the League has signed since their last visit. When the Boston team is hired, the Magnificent Players go to the town and teach new recruits (Jeff Green, Curley Krstic, Carlos Arroyo) how to defend themselves. When the leader of the bandits arrives, the Magnificent Celts fight him and his men for the final spot in the playoffs.

The Dirty Dozen
A player (Kevin Garnett) with an attitude problem and a history of getting things done is told to interview replacements (Jeff Green, Curley Krstic, Troy Murphy, Carlos Arroyo) with death sentences or long terms on bad teams for a dangerous mission; They must parachute behind enemy lines and cause havoc for the Lakers on the eve of the playoffs.

With the best superior officer in the league (Doc Rivers) who likes to butt heads, the local recruiter (Danny Ainge), is being "given" a new assignment, to train 12 men who are either sentenced to life on losing teams, to go behind enemy lines to raid the Heat, led by LeBron, that are using paid mercenaries as a team to win the NBA championship.

The Great Escape
In 2011, the Lakers have built what they consider an escape proof Playoff Season where they plan to eliminate all the inferior teams, *i.e.* those that have made multiple championships in the past. What the Lakers don't realize is that all the best escape minds are now in one location, Boston.

Air Force Squadron Leader Kevin Garnett plans not just one championship season, but several runs at the Lakers. Somewhat outside of the plot are Captain Hilts (Ray Allen) and Officer Ives (Paul Pierce)- who spent their first thirty days in camp in the cooler together - they who are unofficially assigned as the decoys who will make more rudimentary escape attempts,

The Expendables

Barney Ross (Kevin Garnett) leads the "Expendables", a band of highly skilled basketball players including 3-point enthusiast Lee Christmas (Ray Allen) heavy weapons specialist Hale Caesar (Shaquille O'Neal), demolitionist Toll Road (Paul Pierce) and loose-cannon sniper Gunner Jensen (Rajon Rondo). When the group is commissioned by the mysterious Mr. Church (Danny Ainge) to win the NBA Championship, the action becomes hot and heavy.

No Country for Old Men

In rural Boston, welder and hunter Llewelyn Moss (Kevin Garnett) discovers the remains of playoff teams who have all killed each other in an exchange gone violently wrong. This puts the psychopathic killer, Anton Chigurh (LeBron James), on his trail. Meanwhile, the laconic Sheriff Ed Tom Bell (Ray Allen) and his deputy (Paul Pierce) blithely oversee the investigation even as they struggle to face the sheer enormity of winning a second championship while the clock winds down.

Boston Celtics: Is the Pot o'Celtic Gold Now in Washington?

Lucky, the Celtics' leprechaun remains silent about his pot o'gold and whether it will be available for the next Celtic home game.

Earlier in the week, key Celtics players showed up at an expensive Obama fundraiser in Boston, down the road from the Garden, but uptown in price.

The cost of meeting President Obama would be daunting to most NBA fans, but not so daunting to Celtics players who brought with them a pot of gold the Celtic leprechaun usually hides.

President Barack Obama came to Boston on Tuesday night to praise education efforts in science at a local school, but also brought with him all the Democratic House members from Massachusetts, and House Minority Leader Nancy Pelosi, in the common cause of raising money to remain in the White House for a second term.

Notable Celtic Democrat and partial owner, Steve Pagliuca, arranged for the most admired Celtics to meet the President. But this was not really a social call, nor a public event to honor or to celebrate players and accomplishments.

President Obama must raise money from rich donors for Democrats who may be up for re-election in 2012. And, the fat cats this time were the lean Celtics, best known as the Big Three.

Last October President Barack Obama met with Dwayne Wade and Chris Bosh at a private fundraiser, partly organized by Wade. They allegedly paid nearly $30,000 for the short conversation in private with the President of the United States.

LeBron James saved his money for a rainy day.

Basketball enthusiast Obama reportedly impressed Chris Bosh by knowing him by sight. When you pay that much, the President will likely remember your face. Mr. Obama also told the Heat players that he would be rooting for them in the season, except when they played the Chicago Bulls, Obama's hometown team.

The recent one-point defeat of the Heat and subsequent crying spell by the Diminutive Big Three may have been a cause for laughter at the private meeting with the Celtics on Tuesday night.

It is quite likely that President Obama told the Celtics how much he supported them, except when he rooted for the Chicago Bulls.

On the other hand, Mr. Obama recently put in a strong plug for a statue of Bill Russell, another Celtic legend, at the recent Medal of Freedom ceremony. It's likely this may have come up in the short meeting with the President. The Celtics under Pagliuca have begun a drive for a Russell statue.

Steve Pagliuca, who was a candidate for the seat in the U.S. Senate won by Republican Scott Brown, organized a special private room meeting between Celtics and the President.

The guests were likely willing to pay a minimum of $5,000 $25,000 for the privilege. Mike Lynch, respected sports journalist of WCVB in Boston, so reported.

Doc Rivers, Ray Allen, Paul Pierce, and Kevin Garnett either paid or had their tab picked up by the friendly ownership. The richest Celtic of them all, Shaquille O'Neal, was unable to find his debit card in time for the personal meeting at the Boston Museum of Fine Arts gala.

More details will likely leak out when the players admit how thrilling it is that President Obama knows them by name.

Rajon Rondo and LeBron James: David versus Goliath?

When Rajon Rondo takes on the Big Men, like LeBron James, he represents the classic underdog of history.

Where else can you find the greatest story of size beating bigger size than the boy with the five stones: David and his opponent Goliath.

The Boston Celtics will likely face the Philistines of the NBA. Yes, we refer to the new Threesome that want to be big: the Miami Heat, Dwayne Wade and Chris Bosh with LeBron James.

The Heat has its own champion of all Philistines in LeBron James. If it comes down to the challenge of this Heat Goliath, he asks for the best weapon to come forth and meet him one-on-one.

Already during the season, the Celtics have sent their prime youthful fighter, the one young player who is not part of the Big Three to meet the challenge. During the regular season, it was Rondo who defended James.

In the playoffs, that warm-up will likely become the match that resonates throughout all history for which Rondo may write the songs of myth and legend.

Rondo, like David, is meant only to bring assists to his big brothers, Paul and Ray and Kevin. No one expects him to battle the enemy *mano-a-mano*.

Boston's own King Saul, Doc Rivers, may reluctantly send out his fearless point guard, perhaps having only the faith that brave young men should smite giant monsters.

Rondo has already found his smooth stones. With each stone he can win a playoff game in the series. He needs only four stones, four wins. In the Bible, David needed to find five stones.

When Rondo and LeBron confront each other, the Celtic David will likely seem overmatched. But, Rondo lives with the secret knowledge of all Celtic history. He will feed Lebron's head to all the birds of the air and wild beasts of the earth.

Perhaps Rondo's sling shot passes will not always meet the mark, but the history of the world, and the myth of the Celtics, tell us he will slay the Philistine from Miami.

Rajon Rondo Rises Above the All-Star Voting of the NBA!

One day the powers of the universe will grace the Boston Celtics' point guard Rajon Rondo with his own special honor in the Firmament. He shows all the potential of becoming one of the brightest, most luminous players in all the games of NBA basketball.

A star holds together a team with his gravity. When a young player has such powerful forces around him as Pierce, Garnett, and Allen, he could easily become a dwarf star, or like many, a mere satellite of the giants.

Yet, Rondo manages to bring all his skills into the mix, picking each of his star mates out of crowds, passing to them when they are hottest. In that way he shows most of the energy of all the Celtics.

Surely the Big Three stars are the most visible forces in the Celtics' sky, but on a nightly basis, looking at his assists and points, Rondo never becomes eclipsed by the tallest balls of light on the Celtics.

Good coaches like Doc Rivers can determine the presence, maturity, chemical composition and many other properties of a star by observing the spectrum of players with whom he can communicate over the course of a long season.

Other characteristics of a star are determined by his evolutionary history, including peripheral vision, ball rotation, ability to create movement, and picking out the hot hand among his players.

A true star begins as an immediately recognizable cloud of material composed primarily with flash, panache, along with trace amounts of heavier elements needed for a complete "game." Watching Rondo daily with his drives, dribbles, and delights, shows he is not merely a reflection of the stars around him.

Most team systems have binary stars, two at most. The Celtics have a Milky Way with three *bona fide* Hall of Fame supernovae. Rondo makes for a quadruple system, rare in the galaxy of NBA teams.

In Rondo's case, his inclusion or exclusion from All-Star squads is irrelevant. Every night with Pierce, Allen, and Garnett is an All-Star game.

Rondo remains apart from mundane All-Star games where Hubble cameras scan the darkness seeking examples of real talent.

Rajon Rondo is a star, a real star, a true star, a genuine star. Look to the Garden skies, and you may see him shooting to fame without the so-called All-Star label.

Jacoby Ellsbury and Rajon Rondo: Birds of a Feather?

Only a fair weather fan disparages the speedy tandem of Boston Celtics star Rajon Rondo and Boston Red Sox star Jacoby Ellsbury. Those chirping boo-birds may be going the way of the extinct dodo bird *(Raphus cucullatus).*

Like Wile E. Coyote, fans that chase after these road runners may run head-long into a wall.

Yet, once again, an unpleasant word has been whispered in comments online in response to Boston's exotic twins by calling Rajon and Jacoby, "Head-cases."

There is something disquieting and malevolent about the notion that the two young stars could fall under this unfortunate label.

If you are not sure what the slang may mean, you have only to consult the *Online Slang Dictionary, Merriam-Webster,* and any other Google sources from our era's banks of knowledge.

In the past we may have gone to the Oracle of Delphi or *Encyclopedia Americana*, but now a few taps on the keyboard brings us to the Internet gods of superstition, misinformation, and downright base statistics.

Before calling each young star athlete "Head-case," fans need to be sure what that term has come to mean. The term derived from the early 1970s when it came into wider usage among the early drug-user crowd.

Apparently it meant someone not really clinically insane, but on the edge of eccentricity and unpredictability. It has become more loosely applied in the 21st century.

The term "head-case" is considered mean-spirited, derisive and contemptuous. Thrown about with abandon by non-experts in psychology, the term is also a word that may reflect on the emotional or foolish state of the speaker as well as the subject.

Rondo and Ellsbury regularly suffer catcalls by critical fans as "head-cases." It's like Sylvester the Cat attacking Tweetie the Bird.

This movement began in previous seasons. Ellsbury was deemed to be overly sensitive and nearly paranoid about his broken ribs, declining the advice of Red Sox doctors to seek out independent opinions.

Rondo has been mercurial, keeping to himself. He has proven less friendly than most point guards, even to teammates. He has had the unenviable task of directing future Hall of Famers. He was said to be emotionally distraught recently over the trade of a certain player.

Whether Rondo or Ellsbury has deep emotional problems, only they know for sure. We may argue that everyone in the world has some kind of emotional problem at some point in life.

These two men are speedy, gifted, handsome, pampered, admired stars in their sports. They have won accolades and expect to be centerpieces of their team's rise to championship levels.

We may well wonder how many young superstars have been temperamental, moody, arrogant, or self-centered. Probably the number is legion.

Whether resembling Daffy Duck or Jonathan Livingston Seagull, sports stars worry about squandering of their gifts, abuse of their talents, and may work to protect themselves from the intrusions of the world.

With a media gone wild, today's professional athletes are more caged by public scrutiny than ever before.

We may well call Rondo and Ellsbury "flighty," or having "ruffled feathers."

It is that notion leading bird-brained fans to call the twin tandem of Boston sports a couple of "head-cases."

One thing is for sure. Boston's peckish stars are now birds of a feather.

Flighty fans of Rondo and gawking groupies of Ellsbury may want to mimic the cry of those at the Marblehead Bird-Watcher Society.

Next time you encounter someone that suggests Rondo or Ellsbury is a head-case, merely call out: "Bull-finch!"

Oklahoma City Thunder and Boston Celtics in NBA Finals?

Ridiculous? Unlikely? Weird?

If the Oklahoma City Thunder make it deep into the playoffs, then the weak West has been put into a shock of the greatest magnitude: the Lakers have fallen on hard times and have suffered premature elimination.

If the Thunder are on a roll across the plains of America, and the Celtics have fended off the magical heat wave from the South. The Celtics may end up gored seriously by the Bulls, staggering into the Finals.

The upshot would feature the debilitated Boston Celtics at the path of the thunderous Thunder, awaiting a lightning strike at the crossroads.

Dorothy, the Celtics are not in Kansas. It's Oklahoma where the corn is as high as an elephant's eye.

The four traded and betrayed players might have to play their hearts out, against their former teammates.

That's never a good scenario for victory, though it would make for dramatic sporting games. The individuals would supersede the teams.

The ultimate experience for fans and players will be to see Rajon Rondo and Kendrick Perkins, after five bonding seasons together in Boston, on opposite sides of the court.

Their teary reunion may not be on national television, but in a quiet dinner the night before where the lovebirds join hands one last time.

One presumes Rajon will run circles around his scowling friend who may swat him to show who's the boss.

How will that strong professional athlete's sense of competition play out for these two men? They were the Eng and Chang of Celtic lore, Siamese Twins connected at the hip until death.

The case of Perk and Rondo may join the great tales of sports myth.

Now they will become Thunder and Lightning, Salt and Pepper, Dog and Cat. The results may astound those looking to resolve the great rivalries in human history.

If memory serves me correctly, the Woolly Mammoth is now a stuffed specimen at a St. Petersburg museum in Russia. The visitors to gawk at the loser are called *Homo sapiens*.

If I recall the ending of *King Kong*, "T'was Beauty who killed the Beast," according to Mr. Carl Denham. In these matters, I always defer to man who brought us the Eighth Wonder of the World.

Wonders may never cease as *Predator* goes against *Alien*. I am rooting for OKC Thunder and Boston Celtics to go to the NBA Finals.

Who said it? Rajon Rondo or Bette Davis?

"Fasten your seatbelts, it's going to be a bumpy night." If Rajon Rondo said this, fans would know their Boston Celtics transport was going into turbulence.

Can you tell what quotes were said by Rajon Rondo, and which ones are from grand actress and star Bette Davis?

All quotes have been altered to refer to basketball specifically. Some were actually spoken by Rondo.

"I want the ball in my hands at the end of the game. I want to make something happen."

"If we were going to lose, it was going to be all on me. Luckily, it went in."

"Everyone has an opinion."

"Point guards all end up by ourselves. Who knows? Maybe we want to."

"If you want a thing done good, get a couple of old Celtics to do it."

"In this playoff race everybody's guilty till proved innocent!"

"Hoops should be bigger than life. Every game should be bigger than life. It should all be bigger than life."

"I will survive because I am tougher than anybody else."

"The art of basketball in my opinion is knowing how to fill a basket."

"I'll play with it first and tell you what it is later."

"In this business, until you're known for a monster dunk, you're not an NBA star."

"This has always been a motto of mine: Attempt the impossible in order to improve my play."

"Victory # 1,000, if I play it that long, will take place in a well-padded booby-hatch."

"I've lost my faith in dunks."

"That's the Celtics: an old kazoo with some sparklers."

"Pleasure of victory lasts but a moment, Pain of loss lasts a lifetime."

Only the first three are actually from Rondo. The fact is all the other misquotes are from Bette Davis, rephrased with basketball references. It only seems like Rondo said them.

Will Boston Celtics Consider Trading the Mercurial Rondo?

Tangled, Disney's fractured fairy tale, may be the gold standard for Rajon Rondo and the Celtics, as the star point guard has been up and down on par with the Dow in recent weeks.

Be advised: General manager Danny Ainge will pull the trigger, trading Rondo in a flash this summer if they don't win a championship this season.

The evidence surrounds us more completely than a cavalry trooper looking out at Little Big Horn.

If the trading of Kendrick Perkins inflamed Celtic fans, the departure of Rondo would raise a din not heard in these parts since the Shot Heard 'Round the World.

Since all expert opinions vary about whether Rondo is injured, one presumes he has talked to no one about what is really bothering him.

Only he knows.

Rondo is master of his own destiny. If he fails to lead the club to banner No. 18, he may find himself thrown out of the TD Garden faster than when Eve and her apple dumpling beat a hasty exit from Eden.

If Rondo misses Perk, he may well find himself out in Oklahoma, reunited with his pal. If he has plantar fasciitis or some other cause of flat feats, he may hobble himself out of a job on this team.

Rondo's contract status for the next season seems set, like Arthur's sword, in stone. He remains bound by his $55 million extension signed over a year ago, but that does not exclude trades.

After the recent Ainge dealings, Rajon's bond with the Celtics has been shaken, not stirred.

In the NBA, a man's bond is as good as his last playoff series.

Ainge has been emboldened by the success of his stunning moves—refusing to trade Ray Allen last year, signing Shaq last summer, dumping Perk this year.

If Rondo loses in a playoff round and has a poor series, it may be his last series in Boston as a Celtic. Ainge would yank out his Celtic heart in a heartbeat.

Hubris in your star athlete of the future is not going to wash with Danny Ainge. In case you missed that day of vocabulary lessons in seventh grade, hubris is "extreme haughtiness or arrogance."

Rondo needs to understand that Murphy, Arroyo, Green, West and Davis are more reliable on that court in the short-term playoff season than Erden, Harangody, Robinson, Perkins and Davis.

Would Ainge really pull the trigger on his temperamental star? You bet.

A man who'd throw three-point jumpers with Larry Bird standing next to him may be capable of anything.

Any point guard worth his salt sees his teammates as chess pieces on the board. The most powerful piece is the queen, whose actions can swing in any direction.

Only the highest level of play by Rajon Rondo when it counts in the playoffs will provide answers in this tangled fairy tale.

Is this tale cautionary or merely fantasy? Should we fear Rondo's capricious nature? Should we be more fearful of Ainge's wheeling and dealing?

Perhaps we will all just have a good laugh about this during the Duck Boat Parade at the season's end.

Doc Rivers Takes Coaching Lessons from Mae West, and Rajon Rondo Delivers

Leave it to Doc Rivers to give us something quotable. He was so thrilled with the return to form of Rajon Rondo that he called his guard's 22-point back-to-back games "coach's porn."

We wondered what kind of performance would be elicited from Rajon if his coach were the dynamic Mae West of the bawdy *double-entendre,* precursor of the triple *double-entendre.*

We are reminded of the great advice from sex goddess Mae West whose words can be adapted to today's basketball in the NBA.

Mae once said, "It's not the men in my life, but the life in my men…" that got her team going.

Miss West might well tell young Rondo after one of his stellar performances, "Come up and see me some time, Big Boy."

We wish we could hear Mae comment: "Is that a triple double? Or are you just glad to see me?"

Mae would warn Rajon: "When point guards go wrong, the media go right after them."

You can hear her now: "He who hesitates to pass is a damn fool."

She would tell her eager acolyte: "Avoid the temptation to shoot unless you can't resist it any longer."

She could certainly explain how to handle media opinions: "You don't ask the enemy how to win the war."

As for wearing his heart on his sleeveless jersey, Mae might chasten Rondo: "Don't show your contempt on the court. Do your best to hide it."

As for scoring in a pinch, she could add them up faster than a calculator: "Two and two is four and five will get you ten if you know how to work it."

Coach West would tell her young protégé: "A point guard who knows the ropes isn't likely to get tied up in knots."

Mae knew the importance of the post-season. "Good players go to the playoffs. Bad players go everywhere else."

As far as trades are concerned, Mae might advise: "It's better to be looked over than overlooked."

According to Doc Rivers, this sort of talk apparently motivates the young guard into producing orgasmic playing time.

We are not sure quite yet what rituals Rajon Rondo performs before the game begins, but now we anticipate his foreplay.

NBA and the Uniform Malfunction: Rajon Rondo is in New Leggings

Faster than you can say, "wardrobe malfunction," players are dressing up like prim spinsters from the 19th century.

The Union suit is backing up the traditional jersey and short in the NBA, and we don't mean the Players Union.

The long sleeves and leggy coverings apparently were named after John L. Sullivan, 19th century Boston boxer and strongman. He wore them in the ring, either as a fashion statement or for modesty's sake.

Today's NBA players are moving closer to the past and toward the Long John look, and we aren't talking pirates here.

When will they start sporting a trap door at the back of their uniform?

Lately, many players are covered head to foot in some kind of elastic mesh. It presumes to protect aching and tired muscles from exploding.

It also does a good job of masking the heartbreak of psoriasis. This is understandable fashion for players who have had knee problems, to keep everything from popping out at the wrong moment.

Kendrick Perkins, now in blue for the Thunder (not a good fashion color for him), wears black full-length leggings beneath his parachute shorts.

He looks like a ballerina about to pull off one of Swan Lake's grand *Jeté* jumpers.

His counterpart and friend in arms and legs, Rajon Rondo has taken on the opposite hue, usually dressing up his legs in white gauze.

Indeed, many NBA players are now wearing a skintight under armor beneath their skimpy jersey.

This apparently prevents any embarrassing moments on the lines of Janet Jackson. You never know when some Justin Timberlake wannabe will rip open the bodice of Rajon Rondo, exposing a breast.

Today's thermal fashion pulls sweat off the body and allows for quick evaporation. Gusts of wind frequently come out of blowhard fans as they spew their trash talk at players. Players look like they are chilled to the bone.

Since Celtics games are played on the parque floor, installed over the ice at TD Garden, the floor is cold, and Rondo may be fighting the icy chill of refrigeration as it emanates and wafts from the ice below.

 All in all, the new look is vaguely reminiscent of Marlene Dietrich in her famous stockings. We await the publicity shot pose from Kendrick Perkins when he models the NBA uniform of the future!

Rajon Rondo, Jekyll or Hyde! Who Will Show Up on Sunday?

Fans may find themselves worried about which magic elixir Rajon Rondo will chug down before the playoff series begins.

We know the respectable Dr. Jekyll of Rondo. This is a distinguished and silent young man whose self-effacing demeanor hides a will to win. He managed over a dozen assists per game. He could thrill us with passes and moves we'd not seen from him previously.

He could hold his own with four Hall of Fame candidates on the court, and even make himself look an equal.

Then, someone gave him the Perkins pill to swallow. His personality began to undergo a horrible transformation, and before our eyes, Rajon Rondo became Mr. Hyde.

This despicable creature steps out of bounds at a key moment, is cavalier throwing up a madman's jumper. He sits on the bench with a cowl made from a towel. If Delonte West sits next to him, he cringes like a shaky leaf in a cold wind.

Mr. Hyde may be emitting a poisonous gas into the locker room, infecting other players whose shots have gone awry.

Experts have looked everywhere for the tell-tale signs of Rondo losing heart. They have the wrong story. That was Poe. This is Robert Louis Stevenson.

Jekyll and Hyde was called a "strange case" by its author. The Rajon Rondo transformation is even more bizarre and frightening. We have lost a nice boy whom we watched blossom into a star as he now succumbs into some kind of bitter streak, dodging the press more ably than other team's defenders.

The greatest minds of basketball in Celtics lore are at work at finding a solution. Some have tried berating him, challenging him, complimenting him, cajoling him, and even kissing his rear end.

Nothing seems to work.

The monster that has snatched Rondo's mind and body could kill the playoff hopes of the Celtics if something isn't done soon. Dr. Jekyll must return Rajon to our pillar of strength.

Surely some NBA savant can talk to Rajon in his Dr. Jekyll mode and convince him that Hyde is not someone he should seek to play.

Knicks D'Antoni Knocks Rondo

New York Knickerbocker Coach Mike D'Antoni said before Boston Celtics Rajon Rondo's fourth game performance sent the coach and his misfits into oblivion or worse, he'd like to see how well the point guard would do if he played for the Minnesota Timberwolves.

The hypothetical question won a throwaway response from Rondo who said to Gary Dzen of Boston.com: "Everyone has an opinion."

Rondo could have added D'Antoni also has a dominating part of the anatomy that is particularly large and padded where he sits.

One presumes that the Knickerbocker coach feels he must make some gratuitous dig at Rondo's level of play if he were not on a team loaded with future Hall of Famers.

We may wonder: How well would Rondo do if he played with Miami's Lebron James, Chris Bosh, and Dwayne Wade?

Well, imagine how Rondo would perform on the Red Sox. You have a pretty good idea from watching Jacoby Ellsbury. Rondo could steal 100 bases in a season.

Imagine how well Rondo would do playing on the New England Patriots if Tom Brady were passing him the ball. He'd be downfield in a flash.

Imagine how well Rondo would do playing second base for the New York Yankees next to A-Rod, Derek Jeter, and Mark Teixiera.

How well will Rondo do playing with Dwight Howard? That could happen, but those two players won't be on the Knicks, Mike.

And finally, Mike, let's think how well the New York Knicks would perform if Rajon Rondo were playing with Amar'e Stoudemire and Carmelo Anthony? I presume you'd still be in the playoffs.

But you will never know, Mike, because where you will coach next year is anyone's guess. How about the Minnesota Timberwolves?

Rajon Rondo: Ready to Run Away from Boston Celtics?

After taking a bench-side view of controversial star Rajon Rondo during the Boston Celtics game at a recent home stand, fans might cringe.

The experience was like looking into the neighbor's windows to see how next door Dad disciplined his boys.

There was no joy in the overheard screams and intense glares bestowed upon the Celtics mercurial point guard.

Rondo up close was not so close to a single teammate, standing outside the peppery arms up, one-for-all moment before the second half.

Rondo, like Garbo, always stands aloof. He speaks only when he is spoken to, and during the game, only Kevin Garnett, Ray Allen, and Paul Pierce exchange words with their diminutive teammate.

Rondo seldom initiates chat on the bench. When he plays, he can step out of bounds, try a fancy pass that doesn't work, knock the ball off his own knee. He can lose a game with his rococo style.

Allen, Garnett, and Pierce are sweet gentlemen off the court. They are polite, interested, sensitive, and genuine. They are, however, behemoths on a rampage when they play.

The Big Three will all go to the Hall of Fame because of this fact. Woe to the young player who must play up to level of his older siblings. If he loses his focus, there are 3 Big Consequences to sit next to on the bench.

After several turnovers, Rivers was livid, screaming at Rondo, "What the **** do you think you are doing?"

It is not PG entertainment for the youngsters at the TD Garden, but a shocking lesson of men playing for big bucks on the highest level of their profession.

Rivers minced no words on the star ball handler. "Smarten up," was repeated more than once.

Allen and Pierce are like twin brothers, attuned to each other and playful to have an equal in talent and temperament. They encourage Rondo, but may be at the edge of good nature and patience.

Rondo is younger, and they make some allowances. They rope him in when they think he is stepping out of line. They may actually like him, based on their body language.

KG is different. He is like the oldest sibling in a family. And, when Doc says something, Kevin Garnett takes it upon himself to guarantee the words are heard. He clearly has a rapport with Rondo.

Players ignored the point guard's instructions on the court. They often frustrated Rajon. He certainly directed them clearly. Were they expressing passive aggression by willfully stepping out of his plan?

After Doc Rivers sat Rondo down on the bench for his ineptitude, Garnett plops himself next to the silent Rondo and puts an earful into his unflinching head. "Stay focused. Stay focused. Stay focused." It's a stage whisper heard several rows back.

Once before I had seen Garnett grab Rondo's chin, lean down, and say brutal things as the young guard seemed eager to squirm away from the hard grip, but he knew he must remain still. Boys must be men.

Tough love and Rondo seem to go hand-in-glove. When Rajon returned to play after Delonte West was tossed out of the game, he showed the flash and the drive the others want.

Pierce and Allen seemed determined to keep him in focus.

Rondo delivered intensity, and the family seemed happy. They won. Rondo gave them a magnificent game.

Yet, I left this game thinking I felt sorry for a parent with an ungrateful child. And, I wondered how soon Rondo would run away from home.

Special Moment: KG and Rondo Celebrate Together

Perhaps the most difficult sports moment is anything personal that happens in public, whether it is under the eyes of 18,000 crazed fans or the relentless eyeball of the camera.

The intrusive camera eyeball is worse than public eyes. It throws moments into everlasting film clips without context, without comprehension. Nowadays, the camera is ubiquitous.

As the first New York Knicks-Boston Celtics playoff game wound to a close after the heart stopping three-pointer from Ray Allen, chaos broke out as the Knicks raced down the court for one last shot as 11 seconds ticked away.

When the ball rebounded to Kevin Garnett, he threw it towards the Celtics bench and looked up court to the small figure slowly walking his way, towards his lean and mean teammate.
KG waited.

Rajon Rondo, never demonstrable in the most emotional of situations, simply wrapped his arms around KG's waist and buried his head in the power forward's chest.
Whatever the point guard said, Garnett leaned down to Rondo's head and (here controversy rears its ugly head) either whispered something into his crown or kissed him twice.

The commentators fortunately had the good taste to ignore the moment that this muckraking scribe took as an interesting revelation.

What words passed between them? If anyone can read KG's lips, a rapt audience awaits.

The action was like a long lost son reaching out to his *Pater familias*. It raises questions of what Garnett said to Rondo in pregame to bring the guard out of his funk and back to his A-game.

We know from subterfuge that Rondo respects Garnett more than any other Celtic.

During the recent documentary series *The Association*, Rondo himself admitted how he had physically fought with Garnett in the locker room during his rookie year.

Afterwards, Rondo told Avery Bradley that he and Kevin were good friends.

Well, this time, the father figure-*cum*-mentor to young Rondo had prepared a potion for victory.

How long the spell will last may go a long way to telling us how far the Celtics will go.

Boston Sports Pageant: The Annual Garbo Award

Taking a cue from *Dancing with the Stars* and *American Idol,* the new contest features giving to the best example of a Boston athlete in his "I Want To Be Alone" mode.

Given in honor of the original Boston Greta Garbo, Ted Williams, this new generation has shown glimmers of an age-old ability to remain aloof and to remain in the public eye too.

Fans have found more than a few candidates among the professional sports teams in Boston.
Vying this year for the laurels are several of the usual suspects.

And the nominees are:

Jacoby Ellsbury of the Boston Red Sox;
Rajon Rondo of the Boston Celtics;
Daisuke Matsuzaka of the Boston Red Sox;
Randy Moss of the New England Patriots;
Von Wafer of the Boston Celtics; and,
Tom Brady of the New England Patriots.

Categories under consideration:

Most Likely to Give a Non-Press Conference:
Though Rondo often gives monosyllabic press conferences, he also sends the message he would rather be talking with anyone else. Of course, the overall winner in this category is definitely Dice-K who after four years still pretends he cannot speak English and cannot talk to you.

No Show During the Game:
Zoning out while sitting on the bench is no difficult feat for most, but to zone out while playing the game must be considered an art. After dunking a basketball in the final game of the regular season, Von Wafer failed to realize he missed. The crowd cheered and couldn't tell the difference.

No Pain, No Injury, No Explanations:
Tom Brady denied he was going bald. He denied he had a foot injury that hampered his on-field performance. He denied he was limping. Then, when the season ended, he promptly went into an unknown hospital for foot surgery, or hair transplants somewhere

undetermined. We are still not sure how serious it was and what his condition is. But the Patriots are now shopping for a young quarterback among draft candidates. No one can compare to an entire missed season from Jacoby Ellsbury and his baby back ribs.

No, No, No, Nanette Award for Refusing to Play Ball:
For holding press conferences that he said he would not answer questions, Randy Moss has it all over his other counterparts in Boston. He even held press conferences in his new cities in Minnesota and Kansas to tell people he wished he were having the press conference in Boston after all.

Alienated and Alone Conditions:
Rajon Rondo gave his most impassioned interview for the TV series "The Association" right before the playoffs. Here he admitted how lonely he was, how he missed going to the Mall with Kendrick Perkins, and how he didn't know he could go on without him. This performance stunned judges across Celtic Nation, leading Kevin Garnett to step in for an Intervention before the Knicks showed up.

The winner, of course, has been difficult to ascertain. The judges have been unreachable, and they are not answering tweets or voice mail. The contest's Facebook page has no friends.

We will let you know the decision as soon as judges can be located. This year's *Garbo of Boston* will be crowned with a Hasty Pudding pot and boiled in his own fan mail with a canceled paycheck where his heart should be.

Dwight Howard and Rajon Rondo: the Future Batman and Robin

When the playoffs are over, the NBA will feature a new Dynamic Duo.

Superman Dwight Howard will at last escape Kryptonite gas in Orlando with free agency. If rumors about Dwight's inner feelings have any validity, he wants to play with a winner, or with playmates that can meet the standards of his superhero fantasy world.

One name that could be a puzzle piece for Howard is the big riddle of the Boston Celtics: Rajon Rondo.

Bereft without his beastly Kendrick Perkins, beautiful Rondo has expressed varying degrees of dissatisfaction with the Celtics since the now-infamous "Trade" debacle.

How could these two crossed stars come together?

If Rondo disappears from Boston with an early playoff loss from a hand quicker than the eye, he will be into Orlando Magic.

How would the Magic Superman mesh with the Celtic Riddler?

They could manage with a change of costume, of course.

If Rondo has grown tired of playing with the Hardy Boys, Paul Pierce and Ray Allen, then he may be in for truly heavy role-playing in Dwight's crib.

Always a man of mystery who hides behind the mask of aloofness, Rondo could drop his Riddler enigma and make a short jump into the tights of the Boy Wonder, Robin.

And, for Dwight Howard, the transition from one set of leotards and a different cape might hardly make a dent in his chiseled pectorals.

Yes, Howard could front Bruce Wayne by day, and Batman by night. His ward Rondo would provide his back up.

Cue the spotlight.

Whether this new dynamic duo would play their games in Boston or Orlando may be problematic.

If Commissioner Danny Ainge conjures some lucky Magic, Dwight could move to Boston, and Gotham Beantown would be secure for a decade-to-come.

Rajon might easily shift gears with the keys to the Batmobile and ride into the Batcave of Howard's muscular heroism. Rondo has always fallen for the strong Center type.

So, Superman Howard becomes Batman Dwight, and Riddle Me This Rondo becomes the Boy Wonder.

We have no doubt whatsoever what comes next.

Yes, Pow and Wham, LeBron James and his mother Gloria seem destined to be cast as Mr. Freeze of the Heat and Cat Woman on the prowl.

2007 to 2011: Lucky Years?

Rajon Rondo has more than a decade ahead, if the gods of health and good sport will allow him.

The questions that still loom are titanic and unsinkable.

How many championship banners shall he win when the Big Three ride off into the sunset?

How many more banners shall he win as a Celtic?

Will he be a Celtic in the coming seasons?

Shall he find his way back to Kendrick Perkins for a reunion?

Will Rondo ever really allow the fans to know what is going on in his head? And should he?

Does he have more tricks up his sleeve in terms of basketball moves?

How much more can we expect him to improve before he peaks?

Will he really have a chance to play with Dwight Howard?

Has Rondo been enormously lucky, or has fate determined that he is unstoppable?

These essays depict a short span, a few years in the history of the Boston Celtics with Rajon Rondo at the helm as point guard. We expect there will be volumes to come, and genuine biographies will follow. Rondo cannot stop them, as much as he may want to do so.

Like you, dedicated fan of Rondo, we await the answers, and we will continue to seek Rajon's place in the firmament of NBA stars.

We will try to give perspective to the lifelong influence that great stars cast upon the mere mortals.

Gregg Popovich Pops Off on Rajon Rondo

Gregg Popovich knew Willis Reed, and you, Rajon Rondo, are no Willis Reed.

For whatever reason the gods of ancient coaches have given Gregg Popovich the longevity of a tortoise, and like the proverbial turtle, he does not like the proverbial hare, Rajon the Rabbit.

Why else would a coach soil himself with disparaging a player who went out on the court with a dislocated elbow in an attempt to inspire his team?

According to the ancient mariner of the San Antonio Spurs, Rondo's actions belie the condition of being selfish. In an interview with the *San Antonio Express-News*, the ancient mariner failed to give either rhyme or reason for his rant.

There may be many reasons why the playoffs have been hard for Popoff to watch, but Rondo's injury may not be high on his list.

The Spurs coach gave no quarter when he said of the Celtic point guard: Maybe he did show character and he was tough and all that Popovich may have overstayed his welcome, overstepped his bounds, and overreached his grasp.

It's not enough for Popoff who said Rondo is hardly the second coming of Willis Reed.

The coach of the Spurs contends all he witnessed in the Rondo playoff performance was the deadly sin of vanity, which apparently Popovich admitted sent him into all kinds of anger.

Well, Pop, that too is a deadly sin. And last time we looked, two wrongs don't make a right.

Rajon Rondo may need to cross Popovich off next season's Christmas Card list. It seems highly unlikely that the Spurs coach will be tweeting Rondo any time soon, and let's just forget the likelihood that they will be "friending" each other on *Facebook*.

Celtics Hangover: Part 4, or Rondo's Bachelor Party Brunch

In another proposed movie sequel to the long-running series of runs at an NBA championship, the Boston Celtics Big Three plan a surprise bachelor party brunch of carrots, broccoli, and Brussel sprouts and other nutritious vegetables for Rajon Rondo. The plot sounds vaguely like another new movie, or is it life imitating art yet again?

In this proposed movie screenplay Paul Pierce and Ray Allen insist on eating right and banning all fast food from the premises. Ray's wife has packed a picnic basket filled with healthy leftovers from her television show.

When the Big Three take off for Las Vegas in Wyc Grosbeck's private jet, things start to go awry. Rondo realizes, halfway across the country, that Kendrick Perkins is not on the plane.

Dwight Howard tweets Rondo to tell him that he, Perk and Kevin Durant are in Bangkok, already partying because of the time difference. And, Perk is smiling.

Rondo immediately commandeers the aircraft, and no one knows where he is going, or even if he can fly. They detour to Bangkok. Rondo refuses to listen to Ray or Paul.

Once in Bangkok, the Big Three and Rondo meet Shaquita, Shaquille O'Neal's evil twin sister who freshens their drinks of lemonade with water from the Fountain of Youth. Alas, all four pass out and wake up with a limp. It could the Achilles tendon, or just a bad calf sprain.

Worse for Rondo who hates visible tattoos, he awakens to discover he has a tattoo on his neck that makes him look like Delonte West.

On top of that, wherever they go, Dwight Howard is singing "Time in a Bottle" in falsetto. They meet Kobe Bryant and Joakim Noah, who are there with their pet monkey named Stern who won't get off their backs, no matter how much they pay the creature.

When they all have trouble with their passports and visas, locked out of the airport to return to Boston, the Big Three discover that LeBron James and his mother Gloria have been behind the entire fiasco.

Suddenly, Rajon Rondo awakens and realizes it was all a bad dream.

Executives at Celtics headquarters have refused to give this movie project the green light.

Celtics fans may be relieved to hear it.

PART TWO
ANOTHER SEASON
2011-2012

Suggested Summer Reading for Celtics Players

With the advent of the e-book, it is easier than ever to read a book on a tablet that controls the size of the words. Yes, now those who complain the words are too small (or too big) can take charge of their reading.

What does this mean for our beloved Boston Celtics?

Based on this past season, there may be a few weighty tomes for Celtics players to take with them on their travels.

Yes, we see Celtics already spreading out across the nation on the move, on vacation, and on escapes to nowhere. Since they are flying, we know they have endless hours sitting on planes and in airports.

To make the time pass and to improve their play for next season (if there is a season), we have prepared a special reading list for our favorite Green Team.

Perhaps reading these books will raise the quality of play, or perhaps inspire the team to win that elusive 18th banner.

Kevin Garnett should bone up on a story about old monsters that can come back to life: Jurassic Park.

Paul Pierce may be facing the mortality of life off the bench as he comes into the game: *For Whom the Bell Tolls*.

Ray Allen needs to know that Shannon's cooking isn't all that can bring a championship appetite: *The Sweet Smell of Success*.

Rajon Rondo may want to see what happens to a clever little man whose best friend is big and has anger management trouble: *Of Mice and Men*.

Jeff Green may want to study up on what happens to the player left out in the cold too long and needs to heat up fast: *To Build a Fire*.

Avery Bradley may be facing another season in which everyone ignores him and no one sees much coming from him: *The Invisible Man*.

Jermaine O'Neal could do worse than read about an aging gunslinger that does the right thing and has the right attitude: *True Grit*.

Delonte West may want to learn more about how to channel his legendary wild life: *King James Bible.*

Doc Rivers probably should read the classic tale of a man who makes a deal with the Devil to get the ultimate prize: *Doctor Faustus*.

Danny Ainge probably should read the story about men who go after the gold, but find that even with hard work, it can all blow away in an instant: *The Treasure of Sierra Madre*.

We suspect the remainder of the team is not among names we can presently identify. We will read up on trade possibilities and free agents this summer.

Rajon Rondo & Brad Marchand: Endangered Party Animals

Boston Bruins star Brad Marchand is Boston's latest recruit into the endless party life of championship teams. Marchand found himself with Boston Celtics point guard Rajon Rondo for a night of fun, fun, fun at Warrenton Avenue's Rumor this past weekend.

Already within the few weeks of winning the Lord Stanley Cup, Tyler Seguin and Brad Marchand have been dancing shirtless on bars and hardly hiding their puck under a bushel.

Rondo attended at least one Bruins playoff game, finding the indomitable spirit of the Boston fans to his liking. Does this man really want to leave Boston?

We begin to think he likes Boston. He welcomed the draft choices to town and to the Celtics family this week.

If Rondo wanted to leave, no one could talk him out of it. Now we think the greatest chance for him to leave is the mysterious hand of Mr. Danny Ainge. He owns the one-way ticket from the out of town agency.

As for party favors, Brad Marchand and Rajon Rondo could not be more strange bedfellows. The same height and weight, they are a mere two years different in age. The other difference is as clear as black and white.

Nova Scotia and Kentucky certainly explain every contrast we find in Rondo and Marchand.

Marchand is where Rondo was when he won his first championship.

They differ especially when it comes to handling the press, where Rondo must grit his teeth to be pleasant, whereas Marchand seems to revel in the attention like a member of the *Slap Shot* cast. Just call him 'Killah.'

Now the two are partying together. The photo of them posing shows a steely-eyed, coolly collected Rondo, never one to lose his poise, with an over-the-top Marchand, popping his shirt buttons with excitement.

The peas hardly look like they belong in the same pod.

They are twins of playoff intensity, young hotshots who can turn the game around, and they know it. They play big time and love the control.

Rondo has always shown a predilection for those who are just a little to the wacky side of limelight. Opposites do attract, as long as their game is the same. It makes Rondo's chemistry with Dwight Howard even more intriguing.

Howard recently posted a series of tweet pictures of him in various locations, planking. If you have no idea of what planking is, you have only to see Howard in full plank pose to realize this giant is another diametric opposite of Rondo.

We can see it with Brad Marchand, and we can see it with a night of planking with Dwight Howard.

Rajon Rondo is everyone's choice to be designated driver.

Do You Want to Play H-O-R-S-E with Rajon Rondo?

Rajon Rondo loves to tweet up a storm.

Now to the utter delight of his many fans, he has come up with an offer not one of his groupies can refuse.

Rajon has promised to fly a chosen fan to his Old Kentucky homestead, the basketball camp preferred by Louisville sluggers, at Mr. Rondo's expense.

The prize of this offer is not to fly coach to Louisville in the middle of the muggy summer, but to arrive at the basketball camp and play one-on-one a game of H-O-R-S-E with none other than the Celtics star free-throw shooter.

Well, we mean Rajon.

The downside of this amazing offer is that it is part of a looney-toon contest in which Rondo (or his representatives with the point guard's eagle eye overseeing) will choose his biggest fan from a photograph that proves the utter devotion of the fan.

How do you prove you are worthy of staying in a motel room in Louisville near the Rondo camp?

You must prove yourself with an attached photo entry that shows how and why you are a big Rondo fan.

We await the photo that Dwight Howard may send: planking on Lucky the Leprechaun.

Perhaps Chris Paul will send a photo and prove he should be the next Celtic point guard.

We wonder if Russell Westbrook would deign to enter such a sweepstakes.

Of course, Rondo (or his chosen hacks) will never allow that contest entry to see the light of a hoop dream.

We suspect that some fan, around age 10, bedecked in Rondo jersey, shoes, headband, and limelight, will win. The likely winner will have a story more steeped in bathos than a flood victim.

All in all, it sounds like great fun. Oh, yes, send those photos to *Rondo@fantapper.com* if you think you deserve to have a shot at Rajon Rondo.

Rajon Rondo: Style and Grace, Now Add Pomposity!

The last time we saw an outfit of this caliber, Erich Von Stroheim was directing Marlene Dietrich in an orgy scene before the Hays Code changed movie history.

If only we could see the jodhpurs and riding crop, we'd be convinced that Rajon Rondo is the cock of the walk.

Out in Los Angeles to film some kind of Nike commercial, Rajon Rondo makes his entrance on the set like Norma Desmond has returned to the Celtics stable.

The ascot in Celtic green is, of course, *de rigueur* to any self-respecting fop of French art: *jeunesse doree* were the name of the peacocks of 19th century dandy life. They were all the rage in Paris.

If you don't love Rajon Rondo, there is something wrong with you.

Style, grace, and now pomposity! What more can you want?

The new look certainly would put him in the pantheon of any Madonna song.

Strike a pose, indeed.

Garbo, Monroe, DiMaggio, Brando, and now Rondo.

If the lockout has forced players to find new ways to stay in the headlines, then Rondo will outdo them every time.

Oh, Dwight Howard can plank up a storm, and Kevin Durant wears silk pajamas on the way to China, but only Rajon dresses to the nines with attitude glasses.

You could find the same outfit on some jazz musicians during the Harlem Renaissance, but few would dare to play basketball with giants.

Boston once had the Little Professor, also known as Dominic DiMaggio, but never did we expect to have the Nutty Professor on a Boston team.

Move over, Mr. Blackwell. This is not some athlete like Brian Wilson showing up at the ESPYs in a spandex tuxedo, complete with Speedo bulge.

This Rondo is the elegant Cary Grant of a new generation, or do we mean Franklin Pangborn? We always mix up our metaphors-- and our Hollywood icons.

Kendrick Perkins Rounds up Rajon Rondo and Kevin Durant

Only one man could get Kevin Durant and Rajon Rondo to sit down at a dinner table together.

Of course, we are referring to Kendrick Perkins, late of the Boston Celtics, present of the Oklahoma City Thunder.

Perkins, for the second year in a row, is holding his basketball camp in his hometown area of Beaumont, Texas, from August 10 to 12.

For three days, as many as 150 children who want to work with the NBA stars will have a chance to learn from Oklahoma's stars like James Harden and Eric Maynor.

Only one former teammate from Boston will travel to Texas this year. That's Rajon, who would go wherever and whenever Perkins asks. Last season, for the first event hosted by Kendrick, more Celtics came to participate, like Nate Robinson who is now busy thinking about a football career.

This year, only one Celtic will be there, but arguably he is the most important one for Perk.

The festivities will also feature an exhibition game in which Rondo and Durant will play. Kendrick wants to stress drug education and character building in his three-day extravaganza. Autograph sessions will also be part of the camp.

Ozen High School, where the event will be located, is also the Texas school from which Kendrick graduated.

If Kendrick hopes to create chemistry between Rondo and Durant for some future team, he may be out of luck.

In recent weeks, Rondo has made the rounds in Boston, visiting the New England Patriots camp and rubbing shoulders with Bill Belichick and Chad Ochocino. Rondo also dedicated five basketball courts in the Jamaica Plain neighborhood of Boston that he helped refurbish through fund-raising efforts.

Rondo seems to have made peace with a legacy in Boston with Celtics. He still has loyalty to Kendrick, but clearly the two are now on different team tracks.

Rajon Rondo & Chad Ochocinco: Not Two Peas in a Pod

We await a great moment that will rival the meeting of the East and West railroads in Utah in 1869.

When will Rajon Rondo meet Chad Ochocinco?

Boston has not had such an anticipated moment since thunder met lightning at Concord and Lexington.

Ocho has his photo taken with everyone from Bill Clinton to Manny Ramirez.

How long will it be before he sidles up to Rondo?

With the addition of the vaunted 85 to the New England Patriots, the likewise vaunted No. 9 of the Boston Celtics may now encounter his soul mate. The disparate twosome is sort of like Ying and Yang among philosophers of sport.

Two more different athletes you could not find.

Yet, the two may have more in common than Cheech and Chong. In the Grand Hotel of Boston sports, Boston's Greta Garbo may not be alone, after all, in the media mad scene of devoted fans. Rondo seeks an orchestrated setting for a public appearance with all the care of Madonna looking for the right makeup cover up.

Chad Ochocinco makes public appearances like a mosquito at a horse corral. Don't let that mosquito bite unless you like equine meat. He tweeted this week how he loves his fans, just don't touch his a** (his word).

Faster than a speeding bullet, Rondo can twirl on a dime, while Chad Ochocinco may prefer to turn on a silver dollar.

We know for a fact that Rondo has tattooed his number on his back, writ big between his initials and his shoulder blades.

Whether Ochocinco has engraved 85 on anything less, this season will show.

We know that Rondo will don a beret and an ascot in the pursuit of the personality of a Beau Brummell, and we know that Ochocinco will slip into a gold-colored silk slipper faster than you can say Mr. Blackwell.

Rondo is an introvert, and Ocho is an extrovert, but both seem able to convert fans to their sides. Each has an active Twitter account, and they both take full advantage of any photo op.

Both tweet regularly about how much they love their fans. Rondo prefers to give fans a ride during a game of HORSE, and Ocho prefers a ride in his Prius.

What better photo op than to stand up to each other? Rondo has plenty of free time this fall to visit Gillette Stadium.

Who might broker a meeting between the two?

The one common thread between Rondo and Ocho is Wes Welker , with whom Rondo is well acquainted.

Will these two athletes hit it off, or will it be like an asteroid hitting Earth?

We waited for their inevitable meeting. And not 24 hours after we posted this prediction, the meeting took place at Foxboro, where Rondo collected a souvenir football and had several photos taken, smiling in an easy posture with Chad.

Ocho happily posted them to his Twitter account. So too did Rondo. The only difference: Rondo decided to remove the photo two days later.

Incident in a Dusty Texas Town: Kendrick Perkins Arrested

What happens in Beaumont, Texas, stays in Beaumont. It is now unlikely we will ever know the whole story or the whole truth, or nothing but the truth to set you free.

Kendrick Perkins was arrested for drunk and disorderly behavior in the early morning hours after his youth camp ended with a whimper.

The waters have been muddied by speculation, and the mud has dried and stuck on everything from Rajon Rondo's Bentley at the scene to the idea of a youth camp to show children how good NBA players can be.

Alas, the good men do is often buried with their bones.

Whether Kendrick Perkins fought everybody or nobody, the police reports do not show.

Doctors and hospitals adhere to a higher calling called privacy and are not about to divulge millionaire patients' records. So, whether there was a poisoned foodstuff among the evidence will soon become the stuff of legend.

The concept of honor may have bitten the Texas dust, hiding under the bushel of a friend fighting a friend over honor.

You cannot expect to be hospitalized in hot and humid conditions and go out clubbing hours later, even if you have the stuff of the gods in your veins, like most NBA stars.

The best-laid plans of Kendrick Perkins may have gone up in a smoke bomb of public relations mismanagement.

Perkins was arrested early Saturday morning for public intoxication and disorderly conduct, apparently arising from some incident outside a Beaumont nightclub.

And, yes, fans, Rajon Rondo was with Perkins. But, Texas mud does not stick to Rondo.

Perkins had been rushed to the hospital with food poisoning on Thursday night. He was sick enough to cancel a celebrity basketball game to end the Perkins Youth Camp in Beaumont, Texas, on Friday.

Perkins wanted to run the camp again this year to educate kids on the NBA and its finest behaviors. Alas, that camp may have been lost forever in an alcoholic haze, having reached its foggy bottom.

Without the guardian angel of Rajon Rondo, many have feared that Kendrick Perkins would indeed turn out to be the doomed Lenny from John Steinbeck's famous novel *Of Mice and Men*. His best friend, George, a smaller and more intelligent person could not keep him out of endless trouble.

The youth camp seems to have become ground zero for a catastrophe. Perkins did not attend the Friday night banquet for the young people of Beaumont after cancelling his exhibition game earlier.

Reports continue to filter in that Rondo and Perkins were in the point guard's Bentley when gang trouble surrounded them. Perkins was under doctor orders to rest from earlier heat exhaustion when he was out with Rondo at 4 in the morning.

Rondo has a celebrity function for Red Bull at Alcatraz in late September. He may want to take Perkins with him, and lock him up.

Former Celtic Kendrick Perkins Hires Attorney!

Will Rajon Rondo be a witness for the prosecution?

What happens in Beaumont, Texas, stays in Beaumont, Texas. That is unless there is a public trial.

If you thought only in Las Vegas could you get away with gambling, debauchery, and assorted sins against good sportsmanship, you didn't count on the basketball lockout.

NBA players have met the enemy, and it is the reflection in the mirror. Kendrick Perkins won't let his arrest go away.

Since the infamous arrest for disorderly conduct and drinking to excess, the media has grown cold on the trail of finding the facts. This week brought a few new developments.

Kendrick Perkins hit the jackpot with timing, but that wasn't good enough. Not only are the teams of the NBA unable to comment on their former players behaving badly, the league cannot send in their crack attorneys to hush up matters. There are no whistles for personal fouls. There are no fines for less than stellar behavior.

Kendrick Perkins has hired an attorney who wants to enlarge the case, not contain it.

Perkins had been lauded by his hometown, Beaumont, Texas, for his vast generosity before the arrest. It would hardly do to have the dirty linen on the line for a hometown product that had donated so much to the community.

Local police have done their civic duty by merely charging a misdemeanor.

Though a brother-in-law spokesperson for Perkins promised some truth to set him free of innuendo, the only truth is the bail he posted, variously listed as $150 to $300 on a misdemeanor charge.

Perkins insists the charge is overblown, and he has been "suffering from injuries" since then, according to his attorney Langston Scott Adams. This was reported by KII-TV in a news broadcast that stated Perkins wants a jury trial, and his attorney may accuse police of brutality.

If Perkins wants to take the matter to trial to prove his innocence, will Rajon Rondo be called to the witness stand to give testimony?

As it stands now, there could be a media circus in Beaumont, Texas.

Was Boston Celtic Rajon Rondo there during the drinking and fisticuffs? No one has stated whether he was or not, though reports that a Bentley, looking suspiciously like Rajon Rondo's luxury car, was parked at the nightclub in question during the *fracas*.

And, what about the food poisoning that allegedly caused Perkins to cancel his exhibition game and miss his own banquet for the children of Beaumont?

The truth is a morsel smaller than a golden nugget. You may have to pan for weeks to find the shiny bits called facts. There is nothing more to swallow.

Was Kendrick defending his or someone else's honor when he chose to renew his membership in *The Fight Club*? Inquiring minds may never know unless there is a trial.

Has this sort of drinking to excess happened before to Perkins, perhaps even in Boston?

Celtics media flaks would be the last ones to tell fans the whole truth, or anything even remotely like the truth for that matter.

Following in the footsteps of the *contretemps* in Beaumont, the truth remains a fuzzy creature, like a gremlin or foo fighter. Kendrick Perkins has a gremlin on his back, and broadening the legal case won't make it go away.

President Obama Fires Upon Rajon Rondo's Shooting Ability?

Is it any wonder that President Barack Obama has lost support among Celtic Nation?

Reports now indicate he criticized Rajon Rondo to his face at a fund-raiser. Did the ultimate price for supporting Mr. Obama cost Rondo most of two months of his season? His slump worsened after the Obama comment.

Rumors persist that the President of the United States stood up to Rondo with more force than he used with Osama bin Laden. He said, according to sources, that Ray Allen ought to teach Rondo how to shoot.

Obama stunned Rondo, according to Shaquille O'Neal's testimony in a forthcoming book by Jackie MacMullen. (O'Neal was not present, but reports hearsay).

Former Massachusetts governor and hometown fan Mitt Romney would never make such a blatant comment. How deeply this revelation will hurt the President as he chooses to run for re-election may depend entirely on whether the lockout ends.

If there is not another basketball season before the 2012 election, Obama will have a whole lot of explaining to do to Boston supporters. Indeed, Celtics fans have long memories and are not expected to forgive this lack of humanity on the President's part.

We wonder too whether Mr. Obama will be able to draw upon the deep pockets of the Boston Celtics players for more campaign funds.

Some hardcore fans contend that Rondo was overly sensitive to the criticism. Most of these fans seem to reside in Los Angeles.

The usual contingent has stated that Chris Paul would not have let Mr. Obama's unkind barb sting him. That group now has more ammunition about trading Rondo for a better shooter.

More Republicans than Democrats believe it was a concerted effort on the part of the President of the United States to give the

Chicago Bulls an edge in a possible playoff matchup with the Celtics.

After the presidential meeting in early March of 2011, Rondo went into his worst slump of the season. Many also attributed his funk to the loss of Kendrick Perkins, but now the double-whammy of a presidential slight, combined with a general manager's slight, may have had more than a slight impact on Rondo's scoring downturn. Just this week Gov. Rick Perry seemed to take out some measure of revenge on Rondo's behalf when he said Mr. Obama needed someone to teach him how to lead.

What goes around comes around—even for Presidents and point guards. Many in Celtic Nation believe Rondo deserves a presidential pardon—or at least an apology.

Rajon Rondo Will Be the Last Boston Celtic Standing

Celtics fans and media people always engage in wishful thinking.

They ignore the cold, hard facts and act like the season is coming soon.

Anyone talking about this upcoming season is having a pipedream. After a year of sitting out, the older players will be cooked. We mean The Big Three of Boston. The season evaporating before our eyes will turn out to be their final chance for a championship.

After this lost season, there is only one future player for the Celtics remains Rajon Rondo. He must be signed, nurtured, pampered and have his maintenance costs paid in full. He will be on the endangered list of genuine, lifelong Celtics.

The Big Three may have faded into the past already. Perhaps the aging bones of Kevin Garnett, Ray Allen, and Paul Pierce have already been interred with the good they did.

Stories about Rondo's every move, every publicity stunt, all kinds of activities are photographed and recorded. Whether Rondo is icing his ankles after a workout, or trying yoga, choosing the color of his sneakers, or shopping for salad ingredients, he is the man of the hour.

Last weekend he told media sources that he would decide by October 1st what his lockout plans will be. Chances are he will stay in the Boston area and keep his name alive with stunts and activities. We have already seen a commitment in that direction.

He may be the only figure left on the Celtics when the lockout ends next year. Despite knocks from the President of the United States, or King Kong LeBron, Rondo still stands with a future in Boston.

The Big Three stars are fading like Halley's Comet, soon gone from the Celtic firmament, awaiting a day when their numbers will be hoisted above the parquet floor.

Only Rondo remains. He can't leave or be traded because there is no one left in Boston basketball that shines like he does. He may be a miserable baby-sitter for Kendrick Perkins when the big man is out on the town, but he is all that is left for bean counters in Beantown.

You may have to bring in some big stars, imported wine for the next run at a banner for the rafters. There is no shortage of players who'd jump over a Kia car or walk the plank to play with Rondo.

Foremost always is Dwight Howard who has shut down the talk of leaving Miami, but he may be keeping tabs on how Chad Ochocinco is doing in Boston. Extroverts love to be adored. When you are a shameless self-promoter, you want an adoring public and teammates who stand tall on *Fantapper* blogs. Rondo is the man in the kicks for Dwight.

Perhaps Blake Griffin will choose to swing from coast to coast, doing his leapfrog over Kias all the way, or Kris Humphries will walk out of the church of Khardashian to marry the Celtics instead.

Other NBA stars may be willing in the post-lockout world to pack up the truck and move uptown and into the high maintenance Rondominium.

Yes, Boston still has Rajon Rondo. There's no one else after the Big Three depart.

All eyes will be on Rajon Rondo, no matter what happens. He is the last of the great Celtics for the foreseeable future.

Rajon Rondo: Secret Weapon!

For those who always suspected that Rajon Rondo of the Boston Celtics was not quite human, the photographic evidence has been revealed.

Not since the pictures of the alien autopsy from Roswell, New Mexico, has there been such a shocking case to indicate that Rondo is, indeed, an android.

Whoever created this masterpiece of human anatomy must be commended for Rajon Rondo gives off all the reasonable logic and emotional skills of a human being. Of course, we now know the truth: he is definitely from the Outer Limits.

Robocop has nothing on Rondo.

Rondo may be *D.A.R.Y.L.*, all grown up. The 1985 sci-fi movie provided the story of the first Data-Analysing Robot Youth Lifeform, or android.

Then came *The Electric Grandmother,* thanks to Ray Bradbury, the story about an android old lady who worked as a housekeeper. But, not even the great sci-fi writers knew that the NBA was already the purview of a great experiment.

Now we find the next generation ready to go out onto the NBA and conquer the league. When Rondo puts on dark glasses, he begins to remind us of *The Terminator*.

With his batteries now fully charged, *R.O.N.D.O.* is revealed as a

Robot Operating Network and Data Organizer, better known as Rondo.

We still have not figured out what the acronym R.A.J.O.N. stands for, as the government has not released this information, which remains highly classified.

The photographic evidence has been leaked to the Twitterverse, and now the Celtics' secret is known to all.

Old Celtic Secret Elephant Burial Ground

The young whippersnappers of the NBA have already come to bury the Celtics in the basketball cemetery of washed up and hopeless causes.

Legend has it that old elephants walk slowly to a secret location where they die in peace. Their bleached bones and valued ivory is all in one hidden spot known as the Secret Burial Ground.

Young hoopster hot-shots would rather take their limited talents to South Beach, Sunset Boulevard, and Broadway. Death in those cities is as public and disrespected as media can allow.

Alas, most of the hopeful big shows usually close out of town. Those that reach the big venue are often shot for their ivory in the playoffs and never see a championship banner.

No one gives the Boston Celtics much hope. They are dying elephants marching to their secret burial grounds.

The Celtics are old-timers practicing cult religion. The front office on Causeway Street thought they could keep the set together for a fifth year, long after the three-year shelf-life expiration date has passed.

Chris Paul wouldn't be caught dead in Boston green. David West went west rather than sink on the eastern front.

Kevin Garnett hasn't surpassed Norma Desmond yet in years, but he is giving Jack Benny a run for his career.

The Hardy boys of NBA skullduggery (Pierce and Allen) continue to play like adolescents in heat, surpassing the cast of aging delinquents in *Grease*. Pathetic oldster actors tried to pass themselves off as high school kids after crossing the 30 milestone.

Paul Pierce and Ray Allen are now putting money into their IRAs and 401ks faster than they can run the floor.

The Celtics youth movement features replacing the ancient Shaquille O'Neal with his younger O'Neal counterpart, Jermaine, who ticks off the clock at 32 years and then some.

How can anyone in his right mind think these guys have a chance? The window of opportunity has closed, and the drapes have been drawn. Ali Baba couldn't open the gate with all his hocus-pocus.

But, wait. Can we party like it's 1969?

The Celtics came in fourth in the league that year with nearly as many players in the mid-30s as the latest incarnation on the parquet.

It was Bill Russell's swan song, and he led the oldest gaggle of swanny riverboat players ever seen. Till now.

If you don't think history can repeat itself, you haven't cast your eyes on the Celtics of 1969. They took a detour on the way to the old player secret burial ground. They decided to pick up one more championship along the way.

This year's Celtics team may be using GPS, not a road map, but they are traveling in the same direction.

Boston Celtics Rumor Mill: What's Obvious and What's Not

If websites are going to create ideas out of whole cloth, they had better base it on recognizable patterns already in place.

When it comes to the Boston Celtics, we know what the plan is based on past history. Danny Ainge and Doc Rivers are not exactly shoot-from-the-hip wide-eyed country bumpkins.

You can discount anything out of the realm of logic. That does not mean that Ainge won't pull the trigger if something strikes him as a steal. We can likely say that his manner today is a bit more gun-shy after the raft of criticism he received over his mid-season deals in January.

Though Danny discounts the notion those moves were failures, he will be more tentative when it comes to being rash. The man who shot three-pointers while Larry Bird watched is hardly going to become a wallflower.

We can say too with certainty that the return of Doc Rivers is a calculated and orchestrated move: Ainge knows that Rivers quells the veterans and has a magnetic power when it comes to bringing other players to Boston. He can talk free agents into a low-cost deal.

What that indicates is Ainge does not want to rock the Celtics boat.

If Paul Pierce wants to start, he will start. If Ray Allen wants to play with a second unit, he will. If Kevin Garnett wants to be a statesman, he will play that game. If Glen Davis thinks he is worth more elsewhere, so long, Baby.

Ainge loves Jeff Green and may not be as infatuated with the mercurial Rajon Rondo. If a deal is out there to trade disgruntled loners, then Ainge will fire away. He will want value for value. Rondo is not part of a fire sale.

What worked before must work again. When Garnett, Pierce, and Allen call up some free agent and tell him that he is wanted, count on Doc to cement the deal.

Kris Humphries and Dwight Howard are desirable, but like the former Celtic named Rick Fox, they have their eyes on a movie career in Hollywood. They may see themselves in the mode of Shaq with Kobe, rather than Shaq with KG.

Disgruntled and dishonored players may be the reclamation project Boston will seek. Give us your despised Lakers. Hand over the unwanted health risks. Greg Odom, we hear your name echoed around the trainer's room. Andrew Bynum, where are you?

Age before beauty has been Ainge's motto. Look for more stars from Sunset Boulevard, wanting for one more playoff close-up before their name on the marquee goes dark.

The draft possibilities for the Celtics are not germane, but the team may act as an intermediary for other teams. Re-building is not yet on the front burner, as indicated by a meeting recently of Doc Rivers with his old threesome, readying themselves for another run.

All bets are off if the season starts to look like a TV series called *Lost.* You can count on adjustments to this analysis after Draft Day, but don't hold your breath for any surprises.

Rajon Rondo: Victim of a Witch Hunt?

We love Rajon Rondo, but we are also guilty of holding him up to ridicule once too often.

Now our humorous intent seems to have been adopted by a lynch mob mentality. Celtics fans sit like Madame Defarge, knitting while they wait for the royal pain to be hauled up to the guillotine.

Throwing Rondo to the dogs of the NBA may turn out to be the wanton act of catty fans.

In the Greater Boston area, we are all too familiar with the Salem Witch Trials, in which innocent people were blamed and executed to satisfy the anger and jealousy of the local folk.

If you want to see first-hand how the Salem Witch hunt managed to get off the ground, just take a look at the heartless scapegoating of Rajon Rondo.

Rondo sacrificed his body and came back to play and to inspire his team in the playoffs. Now it appears to have been a foolish move, unappreciated by fans that cry to trade him because he is the latest incarnation of Boris Badenuv.

Forget that Rajon has set himself into a painful road to recovery. That's old news to the new brigade of Salem Witch Hunters who now dress in Celtic green and scour the draft lottery for Rondo replacements.

When did Rondo turn into Alice, trapped in Wonderland? And who crowned all these old Queens of the Heartless who demand his head on a silver platter?

When Danny Ainge himself puts Rondo into the category of unsafe players under contract, the hounds begin to smell blood and howl and claw at the turf outside TD Garden.

Like an escaped convict in the Bayou, Rondo is being hunted down as we speak by the unspeakable rumors that he wants to play elsewhere.

Solitary and introverted people who are smart don't belong in Boston seems to be the message!

Pack him off to Salem, where they know what to do to those pesky witches.

Rondo can spell precisely, but he has not cast any spells over his critics. They have come out of the woodwork lately, leaving a great many wormholes in the mahogany career of Rajon.

Off with his head, indeed.

We apologize to Rondo.

Ellsbury and Rondo Suffer Trade Winds from Windbags

Why is it that Jacoby Ellsbury and Rajon Rondo are subject to more trading rumors than a Bernie Madoff scheme?

Why are the two most dynamic players in Boston treated with less respect than Boston gives to Whitey Bulger?

Two Boston stars, so similar in their team impact, also share the disaffection of many fans.

We begin to wonder why Rondo and Ellsbury are targets of a conspiracy to send them packing.

Bloggers on Red Sox and Celtics websites always fall back to their favorite tune: Trade Rondo, or trade Ellsbury.

What have they done to be branded with a Scarlet Letter bigger than the one forced on Hester Prynne in Olde Salem Towne before witchcraft became the rage?

Boston seems awful particular about who will be crowned with a star on the walkway of ducklings on the Common.

Ellsbury and Rondo were selected to their respective sports all-star teams, but that seems cold comfort to the two leading players who must endure more snakebites than a mongoose.

Jacoby and Rajon seem most frequently tarred with the same curse: they are more temperamental than a Michael Vick attack dog.

How untrue. They may be the two most polite and deferential young stars in Boston.

Is that the problem? They need to be certified nutcases on the lines of Manny Ramirez?

Imagine how delighted fans in Denver or Cleveland would be to have these two wholesome players on their rosters in one city.

Why do we never see trade rumors about Dustin Pedroia or Paul Pierce?

Boston has always had a penchant for the bulldog-style player who eats out of a lunch bucket with his fingers, like a Trot Nixon or even Larry Bird.

Rondo and Ellsbury are actually intelligent and sensitive souls. New England was big enough for Robert Frost and Emily Dickinson, but not for two athletes who are poetry in sports.

You'd think in a city where MIT scientists are everywhere that smart athletes would find a warm niche along side cold-water fusion enthusiasts.

Instead, in Rondo and Ellsbury, Boston sports fans have high levels of Mercury, summer and winter versions.

No, we constantly hear that Ellsbury and Rondo will soon be shipped out, COD and Priority Mail.

Boston fans may be the strangest cult of detractors since the flagellant monks ran around Europe during the Black Death beating themselves to a pulp.

To quote our favorite Bard (no, not Daniel), the *other* Bard, "The *fault*, dear Brutus, lies *not* in our *stars*, but in *ourselves…*"

Remember that next time some blogger states that the Red Sox and Celtics ought to trade the stars Jacoby and Rajon.

Rajon Rondo Returns to College, or Hello to Mr. Chips

With the continuing lockout of basketball and with no end in sight, some fans speculate that Rondo's intention is to use the time wisely by returning to the University of Kentucky in the fall.

As for now, Rondo is playing a professor in a commercial.

Whether he will take courses to pursue his college degree, these pages must show. Having left college after two years to win fame and fortune with the art of basketball, Rondo will now test his chances on the court of knowledge.

Many athletes simply turn their backs on education after the big contract arrives. What need is there for a degree if you have a career where you are making more money than struggling businessmen who have toiled years to achieve an MBA?

Rondo isn't in it for the money. A degree is simply unfinished business, but can it be more than that?

Rondo hasn't yet declared his major. For some athletes it is easy to know where their interests will take them.

Tom Brady jokes often that he was a General Studies major, but actually he studied organizational structure. It almost sounds like the sort of degree that helps someone run a football team. In all likelihood Tom will be ready to fix the United States government when he retires from football.

Rondo is not a political sort, like Ray Allen who is likely to become a United States senator from Connecticut within a few years.

We know that Rajon Rondo is one of the few basketball players who is literate in his writing, down to knowing the difference between "too" and "to."

Might be end up with a journalism degree, thereby rendering ineffective most would-be writers with a scribbling disorder?

Rondo has a fashion sense, but we doubt that couturier is in his future. He has mastered the art of fashion already.

When he chose the University of Kentucky over the University of Louisville, we had inklings that he was unconventional.

If Rondo marches to his own drumbeat, then we may find he is suited to a major in social science, certainly, and perhaps in knowing the human mind over the human heart.

Rondo could opt for a major in business, but we know that making money is not high on his priorities.

He could be like Rick Fox and major in Communication and Media Studies, but he has shown no interest in being a movie star, despite doing commercials for Red Bull and Nike.

Whatever major he chooses for his Bachelor of Arts degree, we know that Rondo must soon declare his intentions.

Right now only his academic advisor knows for sure.

Rajon Rondo Imitates Kendrick Perkins, Meets Clubbing Fans at Nightspot

After his bigtime charity game at Harvard on Saturday night, Rajon Rondo and several of his friends, including Josh Smith of the Atlanta Hawks and Nate Robinson of the Memphis Grizzlies went barhopping.

Rondo shocked fans at the game by bouncing a pass off his forehead to Rudy Gay for a dunk. After the game on Saturday night, Rondo was involved in an incident at a nightclub outside of Boston. Someone tried to throw a punch off the same forehead and claimed Rondo was guilty of bad manners.

In September in Texas, Rondo's close friend and *confidante*, Kendrick Perkins was involved in a similar altercation with belligerent fans. Perkins was arrested, but Rondo was his elusive self. Usually inseparable with Rondo, Kendrick Perkins was not reported to be with Rajon for the latest incident.

Never a good idea for celebrity athletes to go barhopping, another Boston *contretemps* occurred not a few weeks after New England Patriot Julian Edelman received a yellow flag for his untoward dance moves.

Rondo did not accost anyone, but was perceived to be "unpersonable" and "disrespectful." According to reports, a man named Valarezo (not a Celtics fan) took umbrage at the Garbo of the Celtics.

Before he could assume the position of John L. Sullivan, Mr. Valarezo was under the collective power of Rondo's personal entourage. They took him down readily, and not a feather in Rondo's boa was ruffled.

Police noted no one was under the influence of alcohol, but that Rondo once again showed bar patrons all the disdain that Greta Garbo usually reserved for her leading men.

The Lowell, Massachusetts, nightspot named Brian's Ivy Hall was in a league of its own Saturday night, and now will live in the annals of sports infamy.

Valarezo was defending the honor of all patrons when he claimed Mr. Rondo pushed off. Though that may be a foul in the NBA, nowadays it ranks up there with a double dribble.

Though some unconfirmed reports claimed Rajon Rondo remained cool and unscathed, a few patrons reported that he likely wanted to be alone and thought a nightclub was the place to meet his desires.

There was no information on what dance tunes Rondo preferred.

Rondo, We Hardly Knew You—and Still Don't

The rumors of Rajon Rondo's demise as a Celtic demigod may be greatly exaggerated. Rondo has always been a Boston lightning rod for overblown speculation.

Doc Rivers never said that talking to Rondo was like talking to cement, as Dick Williams did for one of his players on the Red Sox.

If his teammates found Rondo impervious to their opinions on how to play the game, his GM Danny Ainge must have found the cement wall thicker than walls of Jericho.

And, those walls needed an angel blowing his trumpet to bring them down. Ainge is, of course, French for angel. He has his horn, and midnight may be closer than Rajon Rondo can imagine.

No one in Boston really knows Rajon Rondo; he was the man behind the curtain. He preferred that the media and teammates ignore the man pulling the levers. Rondo wanted to be left alone to his own devices.

Ainge fairly much left the loner alone when Rondo's only true blue friend and closer than deodorant pal, Kendrick Perkins, was sent packing in February. Rondo became more mercurial and stand-offish.

Rondo took criticism and jokes with less than good humor.

When President Barack Obama made disparaging comments to Rondo at a fundraiser where Rondo paid for the privilege of facing insults from the President of the United States, the point guard nearly registered as a Republican.

Rondo could have been big in Boston, according to media types. To such poppycock, Rondo would likely respond, "I am big. It's the media that got small."

New Orleans is just down the river from Rondo's home in Old Kentucky and nearer to Kendrick in Oklahoma. We hate to see him go, but console ourselves that Rajon will be happier in a better place. Alas, his bags are not packed.

He's not going anywhere anytime soon. Chris Paul does not like Ainge or Boston, and Rondo is signed and sealed for the bumpy ride into the soon-to-be demise of the Big Three.

We won't know Rondo any better in four years when he signs another long-term contract—with Boston--amid the swirl of trade rumors.

Days of Whine and Roses for Rajon Rondo

Rumors of Rajon Rondo's departure were greatly exaggerated. At least, they were this week.

As GM Danny Ainge said to the media, when you are as talented as Rondo, there are always going to be tales out of the arena.

Those who may be sensitive or even insecure may be more than a little perturbed to find their obituaries published online. What's worse for Rajon is that he learned this week how many fans and media had him dead and buried.

If he listened to the media reports, he would have sold his Boston home, thrown out his monogrammed Celtics towels, and demanded a refund on his subscription to Comcast.

If the friendly home press were any indication, Rondo has fewer friends than a Tea Partier at Occupy Boston.

Reporters sang the refrain that the upper management actively shopped their star point guard, doing everything and anything to rid themselves of the diva of Causeway Street parquet runway.

Media *blabmeisters* found Rondo the perfect punching bag, and only those who watched his original play every game for five years could timidly ask to keep him.

Rajon does something new and interesting in every game, according to this nameless witness for evermore.

For sheer humor, nothing can top Rajon Rondo. He is larger than a laugh and bigger than small man in the tall trees. His run with the Boston Celtics has been filled with all the hangovers of an affair to remember.

Our plaintiff Celtics' raven may cry out, "Nevermore!"

Someone wrote it over Rondo's locker and closed the door. From here on, the lonely nights without Rondo will be like a passing breeze with memories of a young firebrand who learned how to boss around Hall of Fame candidates.

We will celebrate this ebony bird, beguiling with his sad fancy. He often wandered like a solitary fowl. After his soulmate was traded in the middle of the dark season, he sat lonely, but we are the ones now on a desert land, haunted. A swan will mate for life, and once alone, remains alone.

Is there balm in Boston? Will the Celtics still try to unload him? Quoth the raven: "Nevermore.'

It now becomes a less bleak December. Temporary darkness and nothing more.

Oh, wait, the trade deadliners are at it again!

Rondo Laughs!

In 1939 in the film *Ninotchka* the mercurial Greta Garbo changed her image. She went from the heavy-handed, temperamental queen of drama to the light-hearted *bon vivant*.

The personality change shocked audiences and fans. It also ruined her career and forced her into early retirement.

The advertisement and tagline for the last movie Garbo made was: "Garbo Laughs!"

Now we have a parallel event in Boston.

After the comedy of trade rumors and obituaries burying Rajon Rondo with all the aplomb of George Romero offering a new dawn for the dead, Rondo has re-emerged with a personality transformation.

He is now positively giddy. Might that be slap-happy, fans?

Emerging from a cocoon of five years in Boston, he came across as the light and carefree Rondo. He says his life has never been better and every day is a joy and thing of beauty.

It's as if Clarence the Angel has made a visit to Rondo, or perhaps that was Jacob Marley coming early this season. In any respect, the press and media reaction was agog, overwhelmed by the new Rajon Rondo at the Celtics training camp.

"Rondo Laughs!" The Celtics ought to use it for this season's refrain.

Yes, the first press conference of the new NBA season nearly had Rondo dancing around the court as Ninotchka, the commissar cutting loose.

Not even a visit to the dentist can deter the new Rondo (pictured), the sports-beat writers' dream-boy. He talks, and he laughs. The game is on.

Rondo ran around the first practice shirtless, letting those broad shoulders flaunt their contrast to his Scarlett O'Hara waistline.

The same year that Garbo tittered, Scarlett swore she'd kill to achieve her ends. If that doesn't put a chill into the Celtics front office, then they are not old movie fans.

After being castigated as an unpleasant sort, Richard Nixon transformed himself into the New Nixon. It won him election to the White House.

Of course, Watergate soon followed.

Pooh-pooh to all that. We have a new Rondo, dedicated to the proposition that he is no longer moody or peremptory.

Though Boston laughs, Rondo may have the last laugh.

Happy Old Year, Celtics Fans!

Let us return to the thrilling days of yesteryear when announcers like Fred Foy and Johnny Most provided the narrative voice of happier times.

As we turn the leaf over on a new year, we want those pages to remain uncut, stuck together. Let us return to the dog-earred pages of yore when the mighty Celtics rode the NBA range.

In earlier days of the wild and woolly NBA, the original Big Three rode the parquet, searching for truth, justice, and another banner. Bird, McHale, and Parrish were the names that struck fear into desperadoes from the other coast.

Then out of the past came the thundering squeaks of sneaks of the great horse named Garnett. It was a new Big Three! Pierce, Allen, and Garnett rode the range again, striking fear into pretenders to the Big Threesome.

With a fiery horse with the speed of light and a cloud of dust, fans could yell, "Hi-yo, Rondo! Away!"

Then followed an alley-oop to the statuesque Garnett.

With the Big Three under Doc Rivers, the team showed up the plain teams with only two stars. The Celtics were the forerunners of a new concept in how to win it all.

Nowhere in the pages of history can one find a greater team of champions than the Celtics of yore.

Now, this season with the advent of 2012 come the thundering hoofs of the great point guard Rondo, but the Celtics are not riding with him. They are trailing way behind.

Today the Celtics look like a team that needs a shot of *Geritol,* or perhaps for a new generation, a vial of *5 Hour Energy*, taken daily.

Even old Clint Eastwood had to retire *Dirty Harry* when he simply started looking like a dirty old man.

Whether the New Year shall bring a spring of hope, a last hurrah, only a grueling schedule will tell.

Auld Lang Syne may need more than one cup of kindness yet. Should old acquaintance be forgot or never brought to mind? We've wandered many a weary foot since *auld lang syne.*

It looks like a long season indeed.

Rondo and Perk Find Their Parallels in Gronk and Welkah

John Steinbeck's *Of Mice and Men* certainly retains its accuracy and popularity.

When you apply the story's two major characters, George and Lenny, to the Boston sports scene, it becomes a living rendition for the second time in two years.

Steinbeck's two friends, however inseparable, were diametric opposites. George was small, physically the lesser of the two young men. He was, however, much the brighter and had an inordinate power to advise his stronger and more powerful friend.

For some years in Boston, the Celtics seemed to showcase George and Lenny in the personalities of Rajon Rondo and Kendrick Perkins. They were indeed inseparable on and off the court.

Rondo may have been the only one who could control the rage and aggressive of Perkins. When Perkins was traded last February, it devastated the season for each of them. It also removed from the town a literary treasure: the ultimate in sports friendship.

Ah, but we despaired too soon.

This season has developed another bizarre chemistry of two New England players who represent the ying and yang, the tall and small, the Tom and Jerry of football. They are reminiscent and different from another duo: Larry Csonka and Jim Kiick who were affectionately called Butch Cassidy and the Sundance Kid.

We recognize now the latest tandem of teammates is less a comparison and more of contrast in style: the best scoring machines on the New England Patriots are Wes Welker and Rob Gronkowski.

Their lockers are next to each other and Welker has expressed his exasperation with the bonehead wit of Gronk.

Lately they have taken their incompatibility to the Twitterverse. In one recent exchange, Gronk noted the banal joke that was old when his mother was a girl:

"Why do we park in driveways and drive on parkways?"

To this, Welker tweeted, "Ur an idiot! Haha!"

When Welker put Gronk's avatar on his Twitter account, Gronk tweeted: "You're making that big guy look good. Who is he?" To which, Welker noted, "I think it's Ivan Drago or Sloth!"

If Steinbeck were alive, he'd be taking down every word for his book. We too feared that once Perk and Rondo went their separate ways, we'd be at a loss for drama and comedy in one package. Dramedy has come to Foxboro.

Now on a new team bound for glory, we have been blessed with the star-crossed Welkah and his Gronk: Shrek and Donkey, Laurel and Hardy, George and Lenny.

Our new year looks rosy again. Inspiration meets perspiration, and we are enjoying something special.

Return of Kendrick Perkins Results in Gnashing of Teeth

Slim, trim, scowling, and missed greatly, Mr. Perkins came to Boston town. Meet the new Perk. He is much like the old Perk, but plays in a different uniform.

Celtic Rajon Rondo and Thunder Perkins met the night before the Boston game and had a candlelight dinner together to catch up on news since their phone call the night before.

Once the game started, the two tightest old boy pals had to face off. Alas, for fans, Rondo did not guard the muscular leading man of the Thunder. Rondo didn't have to ask Kendrick to Perk up.

When Rondo tried to blow past his buddy, he ran into a bear hug that would have been a kind of succor provided by the Boston Strangler. One media maven noted that his quondam friend manhandled Rondo. Be still Perk's heart.

Rajon is tough and can take it. Tough love is saying you're happy to see Perkins, but sorry he had to come under these conditions.

Another serial tweeter noted that Perk gave his old partner a noogie on the noggin. Love is never having to say you're sorry.

When Rondo collapsed in a heap of clothes that often can be seen on the floor before the washer/dryer, Perk stopped to pick him up. We suspect not for the last time.

Perk didn't throw softener on the pile, but he didn't drive him into the parquet either.

Perk prevailed, but his team is better than Rondo's team nowadays. We miss Perk.

Rondo and Garbo, Together Again

Yes, it's time again for the annual Garbo of the Dugout Award.

Named in honor of Ted Williams, the Boston Red Sox diva before his time.
Back in the early 1940s, the Boston press dubbed Teddy Ballgame as the aloof and temperamental star of the Red Sox as the most like the mercurial movie star who always wanted to be alone.

This week Rajon Rondo, who has been acting like pablum Doris Day in a sunshine moment in recent weeks, took back the night.

After hitting a triple double against the Rose-less Bulls, he decided to keep the media waiting over an hour before he deigned to speak to the blabmeisters of the Boston's blogworld.

Immediately the dour critics of Rondo started looking for reasons behind his dismissive attitude. You didn't have to look far.

This week the All-Star team was named for the NBA East, and only Paul Pierce would be playing as an alternate. This might seem a rather inconsequential exhibition, especially after Rondo was out for several weeks with a limp wrist. In a shortened season, he has not amassed a few months of spectacular games.

Rondo had cajoled his Twitter followers to vote for him, and he felt like he wuz robbed when only two actually cast a vote on his behalf.

It also came after Doc Rivers came off the bench and onto the court during the previous game with Toronto to put the raptor on Rondo. Rivers was not happy with the phoned in performance of the point guard, uninispired and flat for the most part.

Rivers shot at Rondo like the firing squad in Garbo's movie *Mata Hari*.

Rondo came out on Sunday afternoon after hearing the alarm clock ringing early. So, the Oscar-level performance followed the worst performance since *Two-Faced Woman*.

Rondo now gives Ochocinco, Bill Belichick, and Tim Thomas a run for the roses.

Up to now, the competition was headed by the Tim Thomas who has refused to go to the White House to stand in the background as a member of a team and Ochocinco who refused to talk to the media most of the season. As Belichick often said, "It is is what it is."

Rondo knew he had to come up big this week to win back his title as Garbo of Boston sports.

We tip our hat to you, Rajon, for giving us again a performance to savor: we love Garbo, and you have brought her to life again.

Rondo Suspended for Abusing a Referee

Those waiting for any excuse to unload Rajon Rondo have struck the motherlode after he struck an NBA official with an off-the-cuff pass.

Called for another foul in a foul season, Rondo let Garbo take over. He propelled the basketball straight into the midsection of the offending official.

This was no limp-wristed toss-off, but a statement with pizzazz. It was a suspension to be as only Rondo could frame it.

A few nay-sayers are claiming Rondo has betrayed his immaturity. A few defenders of the crown have noted that temperament and anger management are hardly signs of immaturity, or every player in the NBA would be grounded for the weekend.

There is no doubt that Rondo has problems with authority figures. So did James Dean, and he parlayed that emotion into a niche as *Rebel without a Cause.*

If Rondo has cause, it's that he's had to put up with inferior play calling for years from the creatures in the stripes. He has had to put up with fans ignoring the votes he deserves as an All-Star. And worst of all, he has had to watch angry management send his best buddy boy to Oklahoma's playoff bound gulag.

Because of his suspension, now the trip to Oklahoma City will not result in Kendrick Perkins knocking the stuffing out of his former playmate in the game. We suspect they will have a dinner on the eve of the game, arguing who has more anger management issues.

As Barry Goldwater once said, "Extremism in the defense of liberty is no vice."

In Rondo's case, the failed Celtic defense has driven him to extremism requiring the NBA to call in the vice squad.

Whether GM Danny Ainge will cite chapter and verse as he trades Rondo to Timbuktu for the draft pick to be named later…

Rajon Rondo Turns 26, and the Worm Turns Too

As the world turns, Rondo turns 26, and the Celtics take a downward turn.

Inquiring minds are already at work, trying to determine what gift Thunder star Kendrick Perkins laid on Rajon Rondo for his birthday at their private party last night.

Already the NBA has given Rondo a two-game suspension for his natal day. It was the first time he received one of those--an amazing gift for a man who merely tossed a ball at a referee's Mario *labanza*.

Radio airwave wags have already hinted that Perk jumped out of a large cake brought to Rondo late last night. Another added, Perk was in a G-string, which brought smiles to the two most well-known scowlers in the NBA.

Rondo couldn't have asked for a better birthday than to end up in Oklahoma City with Kendrick Perkins. Unfortunately, the ball movement we hoped to see will happen off court, owing to the suspension.

Rondo could have gone back to Boston earlier this week, but what fun is that? The Perk party had been planned since schedules were announced before Christmas.

A few insiders have hinted that Danny Ainge's birthday present is cooking up a trade to give Rondo--sending him to the Nets to show him how much he cares.

Doc Rivers who once used porn references to bring Rondo out of his shell may be now looking at references to next season. He needn't shop for the right adult entertainment for Rondo after this year.

A week ago the Celtics of the future were to be built around Rajon Rondo. On his 26th birthday it looks like the asteroid of 2012 can't come soon enough for the Celtics fan base.

The attendance list on the surprise party for Rondo has not been released yet, but we suspect that regrets were sent by a few in the Celtics party. After all, they'd likely have to go to Perk's Okie home for the big bash bowl.

Other wags now speculate that the party was for two, and three's a crowd, even if it is the Big Three.

Boston media is on this story like a hot coffee handed out at McDonald's drive-thru window. In which case we may not even learn if Rondo blew out all those candles on the conflagration his play has created this season.

Rondo's an All-Star by Hook or by Crook

Though the NBA has him cooling his heels in Oklahoma City with the tail end of a suspension, the belated birthday gift to Rajon Rondo was an appointment to the Eastern Conference All-Star team.

With one of the other all-stars falling to a case of tendinitis, Rondo has hit the lottery. This will be his third trip to the NBA extravaganza where players are expected to leap over small cars, if not buildings, in a single bound.

Since the Florida city is the home of Disneyworld and Dwight Howard, we can expect the NBA to raise the bar on vaudevillian antics.

Rondo can now exercise his contractual option, sort of a perk to the season. A big bonus always puts a smile on Rondo's face.

On the rebound from not being voted onto the team, Rondo will now fly first-class with teammate Paul Pierce to the meaningless game. Pierce was beginning to look like the Maytag repairman of the Celtics, as the only Boston member scheduled to be in the big Orlando showcase.

Now the two Celts can have company and a friendly face to pass the long occasions of watching silly pet tricks and other double dribbling during All-Star weekend.

We are wondering how the NBA can compete against NFL Super Bowl gal, Madonna, being lugged into the arena by a cohort of muscle men. Perhaps midgets will carry LeBron James in on a flaming chariot.

New York Knick whiz kid Jeremy Lin will also be going to the All-Star matchup. This will definitely be a drain of the wattage of the spotlight for Rajon Rondo. There's a new guard in town, and his team is making a run for the roses.

Watching Jeremy Lin and Rajon Rondo standing next to each other will be the best viewing since Bette Davis and Joan Crawford tried to maul each other at the 1962 Oscars.

Trading Rondo is Over the Top and Out of the Ark

The deathwatch on the Boston career of Rajon Rondo seems to be picking up steam, even as he flies to All-Star Heaven in Orlando for the final weekend of February 2012.

If you want a collection of clichés for the issue of trading Rondo, we have you covered:

However you slice it, the string seems to be running out and threadbare. Danny Ainge reportedly has a tenuous grip on reality—and selling Rondo to the highest bidder could provide duck soup to the starving minions in Celtics Nation.

In the meantime, the clock is ticking. The dam is about to spout over the fingers Danny has planted in every hole he finds. The sands of time are now pouring through the hourglass figure of an underwhelmed and underwhelming under .500 Celtics team.

Rondo may have to give up the Celtic ghost, some banshee whose number hangs like a noose in the Garden rafters.

Yes, Oliver Hardy would be remiss not to tell you "this is another fine mess." The Celtics ability to rebound has gone back to the backboards. And Danny is prepared to go west with a trade (which is likely any place on the other side of the Charles River).

If the Celts trade Rondo in the next three weeks, we will be watching Hamlet without the Prince.

You might warn Ainge to beware of New Jersey Nets bearing gifts.

Trading Rajon could prove a long shot, sort of like tossing one up fifteen feet beyond the arc.

If Rondo walks out that door, there won't be any Bird coming in after him.

The Green may not be in the pink if caught red-handed giving Rondo a white feather.

When Rondo goes, Elvis will also leave the building. The sublime will go to the ridiculous, and Rondo's dander will definitely be down.

The Celtics without Rondo will flutter the dovecotes and out-Herod Herod.

What will we do when the whole caboodle tanks? When you break the butterfly on the wheel, it's a whole new ballgame.

Johnny Most knew fiddling and diddling when he saw it—and Boston is burning the bridges while Ainge fiddles away. Celtics fans are facing a Parthian shot from pillar to post.

And, the Celts will rue the day Rondo leaves town.

Gronk and Rondo: the Men in the Moon

Boston's two most interesting sports personalities held dueling press conferences as the last weekend of February 2012 came along.

Rondo had to address his suspension for throwing a ball at a referee and then being awarded with an all-star berth.

Gronk had to address his decision to go dancing after losing the Super Bowl and then having his ankle surgically repaired.

Two more different bad boys Boston could not assemble at one time. We wonder how long it shall be before their paths cross like star-crossed asteroids.

With a nod to his taciturn coach, Gronk said of his dancing: "It is what it is."

And, in a moment of contriteness, Rondo said of his flippancy: "You guys won't see me do that again."

Gronk finally fulfilled his promise to visit the Worcester Sharks to spike the opening puck. Indeed, with all the aplomb of a man on one leg, the giant Patriot rode onto the ice on the back of a pickup truck, got out onto a mid-ice carpet, hobbled on one foot.

He took a puck and smashed it to the ice, taking care not to whack his barefoot so delicately bandaged.

With all the theatricality you expect from Gronk, the puck broke into four pieces and the crowd broke into hysteria. Yes, Hollywood magic knows no bounds, and special effects are often done with sleight of hand.

Rondo, on the other hand, did not pull a rabbit out of his hat. He told reporters that he did pull his swimming trunks out of his luggage. He was planning a weekend trip to the Bahamas when the NBA gave him an apology present of an All-Star ticket.

The stars share one mission: to win a championship as soon as humanly possible. If it's up to them, the next duckboat ride is around the corner.

The media in Boston likely have no idea of the gold these sporting calves provide. They merely worship at the altar of two different stars that are about as knowable as the two sides of the Moon.

One is open and visible all the time; the other is dark and always hidden. Yet, that Moon is the brightest light in our night sky. Who needs star-crossed orbits when you have it all in one big nighttime event that is the seat of all lunacy in Boston?

Rondo and Dwight Howard Burn Up the Hardwood

For those keeping abreast of such activities, Rajon Rondo has rekindled his long-simmering friendship with Dwight Howard at the All-Star weekend in Orlando.

If you missed it, during one ridiculous session, Rondo and Howard teamed up for a dunk.

Rondo dribbled into the paint and into the arms of Dwight, who hoisted him up like a child to the basket where Rondo neatly dropped the ball into the hoop.

We haven't seen such shenanigans since the last time the Harlem Globetrotters visited Gilligan's Island for the TV movie and used Gilligan as a similar prop.

All this goes to fan the hearts of Boston dreamers who see Rondo running down court into Dwight's arms to win the 18th elusive NBA banner.

We can only speculate on whether Danny Ainge has sent Rondo on a mission impossible to bring back Dwight. Rumors persist that Rondo will be sent packing sometime in the next week, but if he can bring back the heart of the lion and the Superman cape, he may prove that he has out-Cruised Tom in derring-do.

Yes, Celtics fans are now in a state of ecstatic frenzy over the notion that Rondo and Dwight were having a heavy *tete-a-tete* after a frothy brew to discuss their futures—together.

If there is one big man who can make Rondo forget the Perkins in his heart, that star belongs to Dwight Howard.

Though Rondo hardly has a reputation for being a snake charmer, he can turn on the smile when he needs to. If Rondo puts a full press on Howard, the magic will melt in his hand.

Big game hunters in the past were lauded for bringing them back alive. Rondo is about to cage the beast of Orlando. Not since King Kong was brought to New York City has there been a showman like Carl Denham Rondo. He wants to present Boston with the Eighth Wonder of the NBA World.

Those who love old movies will recall however, that Beauty lured Kong to the Big Apple, but it didn't end well. Rickety by-plane pilots, known as media blabbers, may shoot down the epic before it happens.

First Bye, Bye, Birdie and Now Don't Cry for Rondo, Boston!

The Ides of March loom ahead.

Though young fans only know the *Ides of March* as a George Clooney movie, it has ramifications more far-reaching than that. It is the day of destiny; it is the NBA trade deadline.

Originally meant to be a day to sacrifice to the warrior god Mars, Shakespeare turned March 15 into an omen of doom and death. If the Bard of Avon were writing today on the NBA, he would turn Doc Rivers into Brutus and Kendrick Perkins into Marc Antony.

David Stern will, as usual, play Casesar's wife.

For Julius Caesar, the soothsayer warned Caesar of going to the Forum that day. Arrogant and self-centered, Caesar didn't buy the talk that Brutus was ready to dispatch him. Even old Calpurnia was having nightmares—sort of like the Big Three before every game.

Rajon Rondo may soon be on his way to the TD Garden where some hideous fate will befall him.

Whether Danny Ainge's genome ties him to Brutus, only the trade deadline will tell. Anne Boleyn had to face the chopping block only once, and Rajon Rondo faces the trading block every day.

The Boston media have been acting like soothsayers for years—warning athletes in the area that the character assassins are afoot. What they seldom mention is that they are the assassins.

When Caesar got his unjust desserts, they found about 25 slices and dices in his punctured body. After any trade happens, they may discover that Rondo suffered a thousand cuts by the Celtics sportswriters and radio talkers.

We cringe at what secrets will be revealed about Rondo upon his departure from Boston. The waters are already muddier than the Charles River. Rondo contrails will fill the sky.

If Danny Ainge has a lean and hungry look, we should remember that he advised Red Auerbach to trade Larry Bird when the knives were being sharpened. Instead, Red sent Danny packing, refusing to sing "Bye, Bye, Birdie."

Now Danny is one of the honorable men running the latest incarnation of Celtics.

Rondo might let them do their worst if the fates sent him to Oklahoma City where Kendrick Perkins waits patiently. Perk has been polishing his speech to friends, Bostonians, and NBA fans, when Rondo is finally done in.

Rondo may not be going to the Los Angeles Forum on March 15, but Danny Ainge may send him there to play with Kobe Bryant, a punishment worse than death for the egocentric epicenter of the team.

When he takes shots before each game, Rondo's ears are plugged with music from his little iPod buds. Whether he hears, "Don't cry for me, Argentina," or "Bye, bye, Birdie," we know the point guard will go with a song his heart.

Has Ainge Put Rajon Rondo Up for Auction on e-Bay?

Out of town reporters are scooping the Boston press yet again.

Locals have been checking Craig's List for the best bargain, but the Celtics are moving product over at e-Bay.

Danny Ainge insists that he has made "zero" calls to anyone in an attempt to trade Rondo. That means he has sent emails, texts, snail mail, and done a bit of salesman-style doorbell ringing to GMs on other teams.

It appears anyone from as far away as New York knows the scoop on Rajon Rondo. Now as the trade deadline cramps the style of radio talkers, they have discovered some of the deficiencies of Rajon Rondo. It has crimped his value on the open market.

In the NBA stock market, the press has Rondo going down with Standard & Poor.

Yes, we all saw him throw a ball into the midsection of a particularly annoying referee during a game, but Rondo had a slight case of dyspepsia that night.

We also hear that he threw a water bottle through a flat screen TV in the locker room when teammates and Doc Rivers pointed out some inconsistencies in his game. Who can blame Rondo? Someone had misplaced the remote control.

He sat in his car during pregame and listed to Prokofiev's *Romeo and Juliet* to its conclusion, rather than rush into the locker room to be undone. In his honor, Cleveland played the classic piece to start the game this week. It certainly beats hearing Queen once more in a rendition of "We Are the Champions."

Rondo skipped out on the United States Olympic basketball team to attend Kendrick Perkins' wedding, despite contrary reports that he joined the Olympic team to avoid Perk's wedding.

Doc Rivers, a highly moral man, was forced to make endless puns on pornographic topics to amuse Rondo during one game to light his fire (no pun intended, Rajon). As a consequence, Rondo scored big time.

To a man, the Big Three call Rondo the most intelligent player on the team, if not in the game of basketball. Heaven help them if they don't say it.

Rondo leads the league in triple-doubles this season, but the big money is on free throws.

Yet, through all the reports and rumors, Ainge also insisted that Rondo is the player of the future, though he was vague as to whether the Celtics are using a Mayan calendar.

Fans in the know have taken to looking on e-Bay to see if Rondo has been put up for bid and hung out to dry. We suspect that Ainge is partial to "Buy It Now" and the ten-day auction period.

Paypal is preferred, but don't read anything into the fact that Rondo comes with free shipping.

Death Wish Mentality Trumps Deathwatch Vigil for Rajon Rondo

As the trading deadline of the NBA rapidly approaches, the groupies of Rajon Rondo have adorned themselves in black crepe for the continuing Death Watch.

Yes, this could be the slowest and longest deathwatch in the history of the Boston Celtics.

According to the *Wiktionary*, the notorious Deathwatch Beetle bores into wood and makes tapping sound. So, that noise coming out of the parquet floor at the TD Garden is not a leprechaun trying to knock on the bad luck of the Shamrock Kids. It's those pesky bugs in the daily operation of Danny Ainge's dream team.

An infestation of Deathwatch Beetles seems to be knocking on Rajon Rondo's door.

Another description of a deathwatch is to describe a condemned person before execution. Those who guard the condemned man include the Big Three who themselves are in adjoining cells, waiting for the end of their careers.

With Rondo, the deathwatch means that the end of an era comes (again) to Boston. The run of the second Big Three/Four has gone a dog-year five years.

For two weeks in March, Danny Ainge has led a vigil, the waiting game for not "actively" shopping Rondo.

While nobody is good enough to build around, the Celtics GM waits for a complex plan to fulfill. Apparently Rondo is no longer "actively" in the plan of the Boston team.

Danny waits for a desperate team that makes a call that makes an offer he cannot refuse. Alas, the Godfather is not running any particular team in the NBA.

Those who are waiting for the cement overshoes to harden around Rondo's feet may believe that the trade deadline is too far off.

For those who confuse a Deathwatch with a Death Wish, you have only to look at the trade of Kendrick Perkins to learn the difference.

The sudden trade of Perkins destroyed the Celtics a year ago. It was a death wish for anyone who wanted to eliminate a chance at a decent playoff run. The team's personality and personnel died in one fell swoop.

Now the trade of Rondo has elongated with all the tedium of watching green grass grow under your feet. The torturous logic of making Doc Rivers sick of trade talk exploration resembles handing Rondo a pink slip, telling him to go a month or two from now.

Rondo-mania Trumps Lin-sanity

With the New York Knickerbockers in Boston, the highly anticipated matchup of Jeremy Lin and Rajon Rondo featured more pirouettes than you would expect to see in a production of *Swan Lake.*

For the most part in the first three minutes Rondo turned Lin into a pretzel and sent him off the court for the remainder of the first quarter in foul trouble.

When the second quarter began, Avery Bradley took on Lin who promptly turned his Celtic counterpart into a pretzel with three fouls.

Rondo came out again in his famous headband, looking like Mercury with wings on his helmet. Of course, this meant that

Keyon Dooling came out looking naked. Yes, someone stole Dooling's headband, which was MIA.

We suspect that one size does not fit all, but in terms of heads, we suspect that Dooling and Rondo are about the same size.

After the initial strong start, the Knicks knocked the nattering nabobs of negativity and send the Celtics swooning. But half a loaf is not a whole loaf.

Rajon Rondo came back in the third quarter to play one of his patented superstar efforts. He left Jeremy Lin in the dust. Rondo made passes to each side, behind his back, and over his head.

Rondo ended the game with 17 rebounds and 21 assists, staggering numbers. The biggest problem during the game for him was when he lost his mouthguard inside his under armor shirt.

Jeremy Lin made a statement; alas, it was merely a fashion statement when he wrapped a towel around his waist like a skirt.

With another triple-double, Rondo now is the only player to have more than one; he has four.

Rondo put an end to speculation that he would be traded once and for all; he spearheaded the overtime win over the the Knicks.

PART THREE
2012 POST SEASON

The Symbol of Rondo Returns for a Run to Number 18

After the NBA banned the upside down headband, Rajon Rondo felt a little paranoid. It seemed the rule was instituted only for him.

His reaction was typical of the mercurial point guard. He discarded the headband altogether. It was one of his most famous emblems.

Suddenly in 2012 in a game against the multiple Williams team, the New Jersey-soon-to-be-Bronx-Nets, Rondo brought back the headband.

Not since spats has a fashion item felt such rejuvenation. Rondo rejoined Keyon Dooling, Paul Pierce, and Chris Wilcox as masters of the sweatband.

The item must have inspired the Celtics as they began to play with defensive force and aggressiveness. Rondo had five steals in the first game with his headband tightly fitted on his noggin. Not only that, Paul Pierce took to putting his arm around Rondo's neck during time outs.

The magic of the headband continued with a new ad campaign.

The Celtics have made a new commercial to advertise the team's quest for Banner 18, which features Rondo alone. He faces the camera, and the words appear: "I am Number 9. I am a Celtic. I want Number 18."

This hardly seems like a team ready to cast off their star to the highest bidder. As much of an odd stick as he is, Rondo is the bona fide star whom we cannot stop watching.

His headband seemed to have wings, like Mercury's helmet. The return of his headband made it seem like he had been naked for a year. He seemed like Samson shorn of his powerful locks.

Now the headband has returned. The Luck of the Celtics may have been rekindled in the act. Don't tell us that Rondo does not know what he is doing. He is casting a spell and putting all under his power.

Now Playing for the New England Patriots: Rajon Rondo?

Last summer seems a couple of lockouts ago. Back then we recall seeing Rajon Rondo meeting with Chad Ochocinco and Bill Belichick at one of their early practices.

Of course, at that time Rondo was not sure where his athletic future would take him. He was talking about going back to college. Now in Los Angeles in March, he admits the school he was thinking about was Belichick U.

Yes, those tips Ochocinco gave Rondo at their meeting were to convince the Celtic that he could play for the Patriots—or maybe not.

Though Rondo took a ball with him after that practice, he also took the notion that he could transform into a wide receiver. It took a call to his agent to set him straight. Apparently, his contract with the Celtics would have not allowed him to be a two-sport athlete.

Those days, it seems, have gone the way of the Hula Hoop and Nerf ball.

What Rondo did not reveal until this week before trade deadline that he was buddy-buddy with another fashion plate of the first order—and we don't mean Ocho.

Tom Brady came out with the stars on Sunday afternoon to sit courtside rooting for the Celtics. It would appear that Rondo would have given Wes Welker a run for the ball.

Tom sat in his best "Man in Black" duds, complete with black horn-rimmed glasses. Talk about attitude. He wore Rondo's eyeglasses.

Worse yet, the NBA refused permission for Rondo to wear dark glasses during the Lakers game to help deflect the bright lights of the Staples Center from injuring the eye that was poked on Friday.

What a shame. Everyone else at the Center had on dark glasses, and Rondo could have done his Garbo imitation.

As for those passes from Brady to Rondo, they may have to stay in the hoop dreams of Boston fans.

If Rondo wants to guarantee that he remains in Boston past trade deadline, he has found his biggest ally: the amazing Tom Terrific of Patriot Nation. Rondo isn't going anywhere, Celtics fans.

Rondo gave an interview in which he expressed his true feelings, having been a high school football quarterback. When will we see the next game of HORSE with Tom and Rajon?
We can hardly wait for summer.

Rondo Starts a New Fad in the NBA

Throwing the basketball at your local bad referees seems to be reaching new heights—or lows.

When Rajon Rondo became disgruntled and had his dander up, he tossed a ball into the midsection of one of the nameless, faceless striped jersey types.

He received a couple of technical fouls, was thrown out of the game, and then received a one-game suspension.

But in the NBA, David Stern has decided what's good for the goose is not good for the gander.

When Chicago Bulls diva and Garbo wannabe Joachim Noah tossed a basketball at a referee upon receiving a foul, he was assessed two technicals and tossed out of the game. However, the sauce for the gander was to escape a payday loss of a one-game suspension.

Noah did not have his pocket picked like Rondo.

The sauce of the goose seems to drip out onto Rondo once again. NBA justice unfairly meted out slapped the Boston Celtics point guard on his checkbook.

If you want to see the inequality of judgment, take a look at two angry responses to bad calls in the NBA. If you are a Celtic, you will suffer the indignity of being stripped of a large payday.

In the NBA they do have something called makeup calls, meted out with the other hand of justice. To make it up to Rondo, the NBA named him to the all-star team one day after the suspension.

We suppose Noah can keep his salary for one more day—but lost the chance to be reimbursed with a public relations extravaganza and commercial endorsement opportunity. Life is unfair.

Rondo throws the ball at a ref—and is rewarded with the hype of being an all-star. Poor Joachim. He throws the ball at the official and becomes just another thug.

What's a player to do to gain respect in the NBA?

Rajon Rondo and Marlon Brando: Beaten to a Pulp, but Still a Winner

Rajon Rondo took a beating during the big win on Sunday.

In order to beat the Miami Heat, Rajon Rondo had to suffer the slings and arrows of outrageous fortune. He was whacked on the head by Lebron James, scratched on the cheek by Chris Bosh, and hammered repeatedly by Dwayne Wade.

Not since Marlon Brando won an Oscar for *On the Waterfront* has a star been beaten to a pulp to give the performance of a career.

Of course, Brando often took a beating. We have yet to see Rondo bullwhipped within an inch of his life, as happened to Brando in *One-Eyed Jacks*.

We suspect summer games with pal Kendrick Perkins may have toughened him up. Perk loves to lay a love tap on Rondo.

When Brando was whipped across the chops with a riding crop by Liz Taylor in one movie, he had fewer scratches on his cheeks than Rondo had after playing the Heat at the Garden.

When Brando had the burning H.M.S. Bounty mast fall on him after the mutiny, he looked like Rondo on the parquet floor after being pummeled by the upstart Big Three of the Heat.

Rondo may be saving the best for last. We envision a playoff game like the part played by Brando in *Viva Zapata* when the opposition put about 500 bullets in his carcass. Of course, Rondo leads the league in triple doubles, which puts bullets in the opponent carcass.

When it comes to big games on national TV, Rajon Rondo begins to emulate Marlon Brando. We await the game he comes out at half-time with cotton balls in his cheeks to suggest someone has given him a hard foul.

Rajon Rondo reminds us of another 1950s classic, those old Timex watches: he takes a beating, but keeps on ticking.

There's no doubt that after Sunday's game, Rondo offered Miami a deal that they could not refuse, and could not accept. The Celtics won in a rout. Miami was held to its worst scoring loss of the season.

The New Celtics Step Out onto the Court

The future is now for the Boston Celtics.

In an effort to rest the veteran Big Three, Coach Doc Rivers played an unusual starting lineup. Rondo was out there, but the rest (as they say) has not yet made history.

For those with crystal balls and prognostication tools, the Sunday game did not feature a second string of fill-ins. No, this clearly looked like the team that will be playing next year and for some time to come.

It was not a bunch of second-rate replacements. This group has shown all season they have the Right Stuff. This, however, was the first time they were thrown into the mix as the face of the Celtics down the road.

Rajon Rondo and Avery Bradley make one of the fastest and most deadly shooting assist machines in the NBA. Up front, Greg Stiemsma blocked like Bill Russell yet again. On his wings were Mickael Pietrus and Brandon Bass. This was not a team of faint hearts, nor one deserving faint praise.

The opponents were not exactly the Lakers on steroids. We watched the pregame announcement that the Charlotte Bobcats had won 7 games, which did not make us blink. It was the loss record of 51 games that made us think of the 1962 Mets and develop a nervous tic in both eyes.

Yet, whatever the opposition, they are NBA professionals and a good test for the future Celtics juggernaut.

Though there were a few rocky spots, mainly related to the bench. we had no trepidations, as this night's bench will be replaced next season by the Big Three in their swan song divinity.

The Charlotte crowd, such as it was, was a seat of empty seats and a raucous gaggle of Boston fans in green. The New Celtics gave us a glimpse of tomorrow.

We felt young like a New Year's baby, and pretty confident. We have seen the future in this throwaway game, and it looks wonderful.

Wee Wet Willie Goes West

If Delonte West gives you the "willies", you are no longer alone.

The most peculiar player in the NBA who has done a couple of stints with the Boston Celtics now makes his home in Dallas with the Mavericks.

When he played for the Celtics, Rajon Rondo seemed to cringe whenever he had to sit next to West on the bench during the game. He seemed like a leaf in a storm, leaning as far away from the wild wet West.

We now understand that Rondo feared the fickle finger of Delonte West.

This past week Mr. West was fined for giving everyone who watched the highlight reel a bad case of the heebie-jeebies.

During one momentary lapse in his judgment, West stuck a wet index finger into the ear canal of his opponent. It was right out of the World Wrestling handbook for disgusting actions.

Many felt the act was comparable to a love tap. Others felt it was creepy and vile.

Those who think Delonte West's tattoos have gone beyond good taste now realize he thinks his finger tastes even worse.

A Wet Willie is a childish prank in which a moist pinky is inserted into the ear of a sleeping victim. This usually causes either revulsion or sexual arousal.

A recent Taco Bell commercial prominently featured the driver of a car on a long road trip sticking his finger into the ear of his sleeping pal passenger in the adjoining seat.

Since original ideas may be an endangered notion in the NBA, we suspect Delonte saw the commercial that has played *ad nauseum*. It looked like harmless fun between boyfriends.

We are not quite sure of West's intentions in this regard. The victim was Gordon Howard of the Utah Jazz, and no word has yet emerged on whether Howard was tested for an STD after the game.

When you play ball with Delonte, never ask for whom the whistle blows. Just stick a finger in the air and listen for the sound of a fingertip stuck in your ear.

2012 Team Photo for the Boston Celtics

The Celtics took their team picture on the last week of the season.

Apparently they had to wait to see who was still alive and kicking as the playoffs are coming round the bend. There were already some players who had gone round the bend and had disappeared.

The Big Four had seats on the front row with upper management and owners. Paul Pierce and Ray Allen were at one end—and Rondo and Kevin Garnett were at the other end.

It seems only fitting that the two and two makeup breakup of the Big Four features the siblings who are most alike like David and Jonathan or Damon and Pythias.

The Hardy Boys remain close through thick and thin and rumor mongering. This may be their last hurrah together as Ray may be gone with the wind next season. He and Paul are fraternal twins.

The other two were fighting over the seat next to coach Doc Rivers. Neither seemed to want to sit next to him. Everyone laughs, except Rivers. He looks like a beleaguered father who must put up with his oldest son and youngest son acting up again.

Doc kept impatiently calling out to Kevin and telling him to take his seat. Rondo is the only one wearing green sneaks.

Garnett pushed Rondo out of the end seat and into the cockpit next to Doc. Perhaps as a sidelight, and for one of the few times during the season for the public's consumption, Rajon Rondo was laughing as Garnett shoved him into the next seat before the portrait was taken.

This is why we keep photo albums.

Bombs Away as Rajon Rondo Turns into a Super Nova

What's worse? Is it an Intercontinental Ballistic Missile, a suitcase bomb, or Rajon Rondo?

Your multiple-choice answer will determine your road to the future.

The problem for the NBA and the Celtics is that Rondo is all three options.

The NBA must decide, but despite the protests (too much, methinks) of the Celtics that their mercurial star is not that sort of guy, he seems to be inevitably that sort of guy. He is a dwarf star ready to go Super Nova on us.

In a year in which the league has played a strike-shortened season and crammed their weeks into games, the drive for profit has sent key players onto the injured list faster than you can say playoffs have arrived.

The problem for the NBA is that the ratings will take a swan dive if Rondo is suspended and the Celtics are tossed out of the playoffs in the first round.

The league suspended Metta World Peace, and the Metta World War poster boy may have bumped his last referee of the year.

Perhaps the plea of not guilty would carry more weight than a basketball if Rondo had not already smacked a referee with his suitcase bomb before the All-Star break.

That little explosion of throwing a ball into the referee's dinner belt cost him a two game suspension.

There will be no fail-safe for nuclear meltdowns as long as Rondo is playing Dr. Strangelove out on the court.

"We'll Meet Again" (a World War II standard song) was the musical accompaniment to the end of the world in Stanley Kubrick's apocalyptic movie.

Start humming it, Celtics fans. Rondo is riding the bomb as it drops onto the playoff hopes. You better learn how to stop worrying and love that Celtics bomb.

Valentine and Rondo: Together in Our Bad Dreams

Boston isn't big enough for the two men.

We think that it could be worse for Boston fans. Imagine the utter horror if Bobby Valentine were Rajon Rondo's coach.

We awoke in a cold sweat after having a dream that Rondo and Valentine were united on a Boston sports team.

Imagine if Bobby had gone on TV to criticize Rondo's free throws, asking Ray Allen to teach the kid. That sort of thing is reserved for the President of the United States to say.

Can you imagine an "ugly scene" between Bobby and Rondo? It could happen to Mike Aviles, but Rondo? Can you imagine players coming to Valentine and demanding he apologize to his point guard?

What would happen if Bobby took Rondo out of the starting lineup replaced him with Alfredo Aceves?

How many boos and catcalls would Bobby endure if he left the mercurial point guard in the game for the final minute when he was clearly out of gas and tossing bricks?

What kind of hue and cry would the media dump on Valentine if he said that Rondo was too slow and deliberate in his pitching rhythm, sort of like Josh Beckett on chicken wings?

If Rondo failed to score a triple double, we fear that Bobby V would note that Rondo was "not as mentally or physically into the game this year."

How often would Wyc Grosbeck have to say, "It's too early in the playoffs to question Bobby's managerial talent"?

After receiving two technical fouls in a game, Bobby would probably note that Rondo was "mentally bruised."

Tommy Heinsohn would defend Rondo and take on Bobby V probably, saying on air: that "may be that's how they do things in Japan, but it's not how we do things around here."

Fortunately, it's just a bad dream. It's scary enough already when Rondo and Bobby V must compete for time on the evening sports every night.

Rondo Faces the Music: Off Key Again

If punishment ought to fit the crime, then Rondo's judges are not exactly an oligarchy of Tommy Heinsohn clones.

Apart from the chorus of "we told you so," Rondo's detractors are crying out loud for everything from the gas chamber to crucifixion. Who said liberal Boston was against the death penalty?

Marie Antoinette devotees are telling Rondo to eat cake on the way to the guillotine.

Socrates denigrators are suggesting a bowl of hemlock.

Pro-Castro Cubans are suggesting a firing squad.

Madonna clones are hinting that bumping referees is in vogue.

Tim Donaghy, disgraced NBA referee who has served time in prison, may suggest Rondo be given three opportunities to trip the referee during the next game.

NBA Semi-Commissioner David Stern has weighed into the act, stepping out of the bounds of objectivity to note that Rondo is guilty before judgment was passed.

If NBA justice is a yardstick, we may be looking at the *Ox-Bow Incident* or Sacco and Vanzetti revisited. Give him Hell, David.

No one seemed to note that earlier in the game when a timeout was called, Rajon Rondo headed in the opposite direction to berate referee Marc Davis. By the fourth quarter, the worm had turned.

Though many of the anti-Rondo cohort want to bury Rondo up to the neck in a hill of red ants, kinder and gentler Celtics fans think he should be hit in the wallet where all athletes suffer the greatest indignity at the ATM.

For aficionados of basketball, Goldilocks Rondo's one game suspension seems either too little or too much.

Rondo Sings "Positively Causeway Street" to Boston Media

Several decades before Rajon Rondo was born, troubadour and music legend Bob Dylan wrote a song that seems to have been a precursor of Rondo's feelings about the media.

Rondo would surely say to the press: "you've got a lot of nerve to claim to be a Celtic fan." They like to stand around grinning and report objectively each week on trading this mercurial young point guard to any other team.

And as Dylan said in 1965, Rondo could echo in 2012: "You just want to be on the side that's winning."

Radio blab masters contend *ad nauseum* that Rondo always lets them down. He contends the media wants to blame him for their loss of faith, but Rondo knows the media well enough to say they had no faith to begin with.

Rondo could easily sing along with Dylan: "Do you take me for such a fool to think I'd make contact with the one who tries to hide what he don't know to begin with?"

If the lyrics of "Positively 4th Street" sting sports bloggers, Rondo could prove that they say 'hello' and 'good luck,' but never mean it.

When the press gathered round him before the playoff game to try to force a sound byte for the evening news, Rondo might have quoted Dylan again: "No, I do not feel that good when I see the heartbreaks you embrace."

Dylan certainly seemed to be singing about the Boston media when he said: "Now I know you're dissatisfied with your position and your place. Don't you understand? It's not my problem."

If Rondo seemed standoffish and downright unfriendly to the members of the 4th Estate, it may be because they live off 4th Street, negatively.

As Dylan put it so well decades ago, "Yes, I wish that for just one time you could stand inside my shoes. You'd know what a drag it is to see you."

Rondo may simply be too polite to sing these lyrics to the Boston media, (with apologies to Bob Dylan).

Rondo and Teddy: Boston Has Seen It All Before...

The temperament, arrogance, and stubborn attitude recently displayed by Rajon Rondo is nothing new in Boston.

Back in the 1940s, the young hotshot of Boston was known as the Garbo of the Dugout. His name was Teddy Ballgame, the Splendid Splinter. He had a few run-ins with the press who would have banished him to New York for a guy named DiMaggio any day of the week.

Yes, Ted Williams did not like the press, but he even had his moments with the fans.

So far, we have not seen Rondo giving a flying finger to the crowds. Nor has he taken umbrage at their attitude and sent some off spittoon bodily fluids fly.

Yes, Ted Williams did all the aforementioned. He was fined and never tipped his hat to the adoring masses.

Ted did not rollerblade, did not win a world championship, and was a World War II and Korean War veteran who flew dangerous missions.

The only press member that had appeal to Ted was the one who knew something about fishing. In 1940 Ted even dressed up like Huck Finn and posed for the Boston papers in an effort to rehab his image.

It was already too late. He was accused of taking batting practice and hitting fungo balls into fans walking in the stands that had heckled him.

Ted also gave time and effort to his favorite charity. He was the first athlete to associate his name with a children's group, the Jimmy Fund. He made it a lifetime mission.

Rondo too seems more than willing to bend over backwards for children.

Unlike Rondo, Teddy Ballgame was gracious, polite, and ever considerate to the umpires. He did not curse them, argue with them, or throw a ball at one.

Yet, we feel that Boston has a sense of deju vu all over again.

If anyone is channeling the spirit of Ted Williams, it is definitely Rajon Rondo.

Rondo Names That Tune in Two Notes

Following in the vocal patterns of Shaquille O'Neal and Carlos Arroyo, Rajon Rondo has announced to the world (via Global Grind.com) that he can sing in the rain.

Not your usual bebop/hiphop *artiste,* Rondo insists that his *métier* is R&B, and he will provide musical prowess with an accompanying female singer who prefers to remain under a paper bag hat to date.

When asked about the distaff side, Rondo gave the curt answer that revealed little more than a coin flip response. "You know a good woman when you see one." We presume he has seen one.
We are not sure if this rules out Madonna.

So, with that, we came to realize that Rondo (a musical name in and of itself) would hardly be singing the aria "La Donna e Mobile." No champagne glasses will be shattered with his *oeuvre.*

If you are wondering about musical training, you need look no farther than the shower stall in the Celtics locker room. CD producers are easy to find when the star is ready to bankroll the orchestra.

Ray Charles had to be paid in ones to be sure he wasn't being cheated. We are not sure how many ones Rondo will see after singing "Stormy Weather."

We suspect Rondo's secret single will be something on the order of Peaches and Herb.

In our wildest humming, we envision ourselves stuck in traffic on the way to the TD Garden while listening to Rondo and his mysterious guest artist crooning like Patti LaBelle and Michael McDonald, wailing about being "On Our Own."

This season has brought overlarge headphones to the ears of Rondo during his pregame warmups. No more little buds for him.

The guard insists he wants calming tunes in his head before he musters up the angst to follow the bouncing ball or do the bump and grind on the court.

Can the "Rondo Xmas Album" be far behind?

Augurs Tell the Tale of Rondo and Pierce

When a long-time fan asks us, how do you know whether the Celtics can win the game? We answer (brimming with considerable confidence) after making precise observations and logical deductions.

In the first five minutes, all answers are available.

When Paul Pierce wears the team's green sneakers for the night, it means Rondo must wear the headband. This means both are planning a monster game.

Let's face it, fans. There is a superstitious factor involved with the leprechaun team in Boston. Only one player can wear green sneakers in each game.

Sometimes Rondo wears the green sneakers and does not don a headband. This is usually a sign that he is aiming for a mere double-double.

If Pierce is wearing the green sneakers, he is thinking of a scoring record. And, Rondo wants more assists than the opposing starters.

When the Celtics bench riders are waving towels within the opening seconds, there is a sense of energy.

If Ray Allen comes off the bench early to a standing ovation, you have another augur of positive foreshadowing.

If Kevin Garnett races down the middle of the court to score like a 25-year old, you have a problem in Atlanta.

When Rajon Rondo is making an assist for every score, the opponent may be in trouble.

Of course, it always helps to have an opponent in panic mode, turning over the ball and making stressful mistakes.

We always risk the danger of being called wrong by the end of the game. However, like Sherlock Holmes, we haven't yet missed a Celtic game when the dog did not bark in the night.

There is a Celtics victory in the air. The first five minutes tells us all.

Mitt Romney is a Celtic

Mitt Romney continues to barnstorm the Boston sports teams, though lining up the votes of these millionaire athletes may be next to impossible.

Despite the fact that most of the Celtics players have attended fund raisers for the likely opponent of Mitt in the fall election classic, Mr. Romney seemed quite enthusiastic about the basketball franchise.

Indeed, after President Obama criticized Rajon Rondo to his face at their last fundraiser, we wonder if Mitt may be tapping into the angry voters on the Celtics team.

Just a few short weeks ago, Mitt was at Fenway Park for the Patriots' Day early morning game. The Marathon was ending a few blocks away, and this day off from campaigning seemed ideal.

Yet, we think it was the best photo op a presidential nominee could want. There was Mitt, looking all relaxed and like your average guy who makes $300 million per year, hobnobbing with the likes of New England Patriots owner Robert Kraft.

At least we know Mitt can afford those loge boxes on the third base side that he is fond of sitting in at Fenway. It may be that the angle puts him on camera for every right-handed batter.

Now we had the pleasure (and so did Mitt) on watching the Boston Celtics trash the Atlanta Hawks at the TD Garden.

This time he sat about a dozen rows behind the former Democratic candidate and part owner of the Celtics, fellow millionaire Steve Pagliuca.

Mitt is an avid Boston sports fan, and once served as governor of the great Commonwealth of Massachusetts.

We keep wondering why he never bought into one of the major franchises in Boston. There were ample opportunities and money to be made.

Sitting with his wife Ann, Governor Romney held up a towel with the green logo "I am a Celtic."

We suspect he lost a few votes in Atlanta last night.

Rondo Explodes for a Slam Dunk

Rajon Rondo may be looking for some anger management classes in the off-season.

From across a crowded hallway waiting for his time at the interview podium, Rondo spotted a film cameraman with his red light on. Someone pushed the button and the ICBM came out of the silo and directly at the target.

It took more than ten paces to reach the offending party, whence Rajon Rondo got into the grill of said cameraman and informed him, apparently, for a second time, "not to film me."

Not since Greta Garbo walked off the movie set because her checkered black and white dress with the orange collar clashed with the klieg lights has there been such a scene.

Mr. Rondo on the attack is not a pretty sight. We'd rather face an army of Grace Jones clones on the march.

A little tense, Rondo was waiting for his big moment in the spotlight. He had to face the NBA press conference and discuss his bonehead play to end the game. It was not a pretty night for the triple-double machine, and his nerves were frayed.

Cameramen everywhere now realize it is they who should be frayed. Very frayed.

The hostile outbursts from Rondo are now coming with more frequency and more regularity. Without Kendrick Perkins to defuse the situation, we worry about the next explosion.

If you like your drama on the order of Anne Boleyn (or is that Mata Hari?) facing the executioners, you can't beat watching Rajon Rondo in the final reel—or postgame interview.

Rondo Overexposed by Blow Up

The best way to force Rajon Rondo to become a whirling dervish on the court is to make all the Atlanta Hawk players come out onto the court while they carry video cameras.

The Celtics looked sluggish and ready to be sent to the darkroom with a fistful of negatives.

Then suddenly Celtics should told Rondo that he was being filmed secretly and without his permission by iPhones by the Atlanta media.

Rondo went on a binge, shooting up a couple of rolls of film out of anger.

That flash you saw during the photo op may seem to come from Rondo's eyes, but nine times out of ten it's a fan cam in the stands.

With Avery Bradley suffering shoulder issues, Ray Allen with bone spurs, Paul Pierce with knee problems, Doc found a new way to motivate his mercurial star Rondo. And, he may ask him to pose one more time.

Doc Rivers led the crowd in a chant, "Smile! You're on Candid Camera!" to see if that causes flames to pour out of Rondo's nostrils.

As we recall, actress Norma Desmond fretted egregiously about all those cameras waiting on her. It took a while, but she finally mustered up the energy to say, "I'm ready for my closeup now, Mr. DeMille."

Rondo has spent hours in the dressing room, fretting before the mirror before the big game. Would he be ready for his closeup?

We know so, but we also remember with a bit of queasiness that Norma Desmond was carted off to the looney bin as she made her way into the bright lights.

Nobody dared to ask Rondo to say, "Cheese," during halftime unless they want to be the next wheel of Swiss cheese. You never know what *f-stop* Rondo will call for.

When Rondo poses for the centerfold for *Playgirl,* we will know that his camera shy personality has been cured.

In the meantime, Rajon has blown up the wallet-size snapshot of Josh Smith and photo-shopped the rest of the Atlanta Hawks.

Next *f-stop* is Philadelphia.

Every Game with the Celtics is an Old Timers Game

We expect that Rajon Rondo will read the classic, ageless poem entitled "Rime of the Ancient Mariner," at Kevin Garnett's 36th birthday party next week.

We are not sure if Rajon Rondo (with his Nikon D 3600) has already shot the albatross hanging around the team's neck and has used it as a decoration model for KG's birthday cake.

Garnett is so old he is beginning to look like one of the ancient stone carvings at the Mayan Hub of Tikal. We have to remember he is one of the living ancient monuments in Celtics Hub.

The epic poem depicts the long voyage across the deep ocean where you thirst for a championship, but the water everywhere contains not a drop to drink.

It seems like the playoffs to literary experts.

Garnett said that he appreciated all the references to aging because it motivates him "though I don't read your column."

He doesn't know what he is missing, but then again by 36, most people have done it all and can't remember they've done it.

We hesitate to remind him that Marilyn Monroe never made it past age 36, and they still make movies about her legendary playoff games.

If being aged and passionate seem to be disparate characteristics, the Ancient Celtic truly seems to be Tommy Heinsohn who has given a recounting of the ancient wars of Philadelphia and Boston in basketball lore.

If there is anything possible, it is for the old man to fight the sea with nobility on this last voyage of champions.

We are reminded too of old crabby Mary Carson in *The Thornbirds*. She had the hubris in her old age to fall in love with a young priest.
At her birthday party, the ancient girl made a play for him.

She got what she wanted, showing more passion than anyone could expect from an oldster. Her old body mocked her young feelings, but she played the game to the hilt.

Kevin Garnett won't be the oldest guy at the party, but he will be playing Father Time one-on-one.

Rip Van Rondo Dreams of Playoff Victory

Rondo was cranky before the first game against the Philadelphia Seventy-Sixers. He had missed his pregame nap.

Rondo is always at his most mercurial when he misses nap-time at his crib. We are sure Rondo will tell you that playoff games are the annoying time between naps.

Sleep deprivation is a terrible thing, especially when you have to face the bright lights and cameras.

Rondo told assorted media in his sleepiest voice that he knew not what might come forth after missing his power nap. The Truth likely was brewing coffee, and Sugar Ray was adding his own spoonful of sweetness.

Rondo must have put some drops in his eyes to get the red out, but his little Green men knew he was still the leader to follow.

During the first-half the Celtics looked like the Roswell crash.

During the first half Rajon Rondo wandered about like a sleep-walking extra-terrestrial, looking for a phone to call home.

Then with the half-time break, Rip Van Rondo was able to catch 40 winks in the locker room.

When he returned, he was refreshed. He began to lead the Celtics against the trombone slide of the 76ers.

No longer looking like your average 'Sleepy-Time Gal,' Rondo was suddenly able to amass yet another staggering triple-double, his eighth in playoff games.

Fans who said after the first half, "Wake me when it's over," won't need no-doze when Game 2 rolls around. We sincerely hope that Rondo doesn't nod off during the next game and continues to have REM dreams.

No Horsing Around: Paul Pierce is on Bronco Garnett

Paul Pierce said it: "We're gonna ride Kevin Garnett all the way."

Hi-yo, Silver, away!

The winning Big Ticket has become the "Rocking Horse Winner."

Not since Troy has there been such excitement over a giant gift to the fans.

As we recall, there were a bunch of men inside the wooden horse, waiting for the chance to come out and show the City of Brotherly Love the way to the loser's circle.

The Celtics are tossing oats to KG and letting their little jockey, nicknamed Shorty Rondo, take the reins and ride the Green Seabiscuit all the way to San Antonio, if necessary.

War Horse should have been the Best Picture of the Year, in honor of Kevin Garnett.

If champion thoroughbreds have been more disrespected, we cannot find one at the trough. Trashed by an Atlanta owner, receiving no votes for season MVP, the old gray nag is more than he used to be.

To the neigh-sayers, we can only chomp at the bit. Bring on those polo pony Sixers. Paul Revere's patriotic horse was named Kevin.

Our champeen horse is the son of Black Beauty and Fury.

Rajon is hitching up the surrey with the fringe on top and taking us along the Mohawk Trail blazed by Trigger Pierce and Champion Allen.

The Celtics have not yet met a broncobuster who can tame the wild bunch. Tom Mix may have had a wonder horse, but Boston Celtics will still saddle up KG.

In *Christmas Story,* Mom claimed the name of the Lone Ranger's nephew's horse was Victor. Actually it was Garnett. He rode to Victory.

Assist Machine Rajon Rondo Breaks Down the Game

The breakdown of the Celtics big guys has happened right on schedule. Worse than the heartbreak of psoriasis, this brittle bone syndrome, usually found in Golden Agers, has hit the starting lineup.

Of course, no one expects Assist Machine Rajon Rondo to break down and refuse to share the ball in the most pivotal moment of a tied game with seconds left as future Hall of Famer teammates hobble around.

All season Doc Rivers said he wanted to rest his older players so they'd be able to play in the big games of the playoffs. Well, he never rested them. But, they were not done in by lack of rest.

Guess what? The historical inevitability factor has joined the multifactorial reasons why the parquet floor of the Garden may not be long for the playoffs.

We have looked high and low for a Magic Bullet, a magic cream, or a Magic Johnson.

The Celtics have not signed David Copperfield to perform his greatest magic trick. As a result, the Celtics are about to be sawed in half by amateurs.

We may be getting ready for the iceberg dead ahead.

Fans are dancing in the main ballroom as though it were 2007 all over again, but the band is about to play "American Pie,' and the levy may be dry.

The Celtics D-day is closer to the anniversary of the Hindenburg crash than to the duck boat parade in Boston.

It may be time to cue the Fat Lady and tell Gino, the dancing fool from Celtics good luck video, to step aside.

Gunga Din may be ready for that final bugle call.

That Philly Stake may be in the Celtics's heart.

Ray Allen will be wearing the Denver boot, and Avery Bradley is veering off the road on the soft shoulder.

Paul Pierce has been pricing knee replacements at Mass. General Hospital.

Worst of all, ball hog Rajon Rondo dresses in the notorious Loki costume on the way to the Garden. He won't pass for an assist and saves the key shot for his own book of heroes. He misses.

The Avengers are bound to show up for the next game.

Boston Celtics at the O.K. Corral

Doc Rivers cannot take a Holiday at the O.K. Corral for the Philly series.

Those famous gunslinger brothers, Wyatt Pierce and Ray Earp, must be ready for the Philadelphia version of the Ike Clanton gang.

We always have more confidence when the Good Guys are played by Kurt Russell and Kevin Costner, but in this version we need a Bill Russell to go with our Kevin Garnett.

The Celtics may be a team "too tough to die," but we've seen similar words on the tombstones of other Celtics teams. The second game loss isn't a nail in the coffin, but it certainly lines the casket's interior with silk.

When the Big Four march down the parquet to meet the awaiting black hats from Philly, we know our gang is more than Okay—even without Alfalfa and Spanky.

Kevin Garnett is making more like Clint as the Man with No Name or MVP votes. He has a fistful of points and is shooting up the town. He's the long arm of the law in Boston.

This time he is traveling with Avery the Kid whose shoulder is in a sling.

If the Sixer shooters are the gang that could shoot straight, they may be big trouble at the Corral.

It looks like the Man in Black, Shorty Rondo wants to make like John Wayne. His response to a Philly shootout: "That'll be the Day" begins to sound like whistling past the graveyard.

The Celtics are in a foxhole. It's time to praise the Doc, and pass the ball!

Scrooge and Rondo Share the Ball

Scrooge at his worst was unwilling to share the wealth with the tired, poor, disadvantaged, and even those with shoulder problems, bone spurs, and sprained knees.

Rajon Rondo may not bless every one in a similar way.

Knowing the sensitivity of Rajon, few players are hardly willing to call the one man who leads the world in assists a ball hog. It seems inconceivable.

Ray Allen, three-point record holder, understated after the playoff game that got away that there was a problem with sharing the ball.

When Rondo gives out assists and anoints the right player to hit the winning shot, fans celebrate like they have found another tax deduction.

Those hungry players at the shelter may feel like they have been skipped over for the latest helping of gruel.

Yet, when push came to shove, Rondo shoved aside his future Hall of Fame mates to take the glory upon his own mantle. If Garnett, Pierce, and Allen, like Oliver Twist, wanted "more, sir," they have found their bowls empty.

Alas, the water Rondo walks upon will start to swamp his baby stroller now and then.

Dribbling is like treading water. When the life preserver was thrown to Rondo, he said, "Bah! Humbug."

One day in the dark future, Rajon Rondo may find himself visited by the Ghost of Playoffs Past, and he will have to look at his past attitude. It will be too late for him and for winning a championship.

The Celtics need redemption now.

Green Sneakers or Green Eggs: The Yoke is on the Celtics

Biggest team decision before each playoff game may be the bestowing of the Shoes of the Leprechaun by the Boston Celtics.

In Rome, the Cardinals decide on who wears the Shoes of the Fisherman, but the Celtics decide on who wears the green sneakers.

Only one player per game is elected to the elevated shoes.

We would love to be in on the pregame discussion. On various nights we have seen Rondo in the green sneaks, but mostly there is Paul Pierce in the neon green shoes.

On some nights Ray Allen will tend toward the half and half green shoes.

We have not determined yet the tribal powwow that votes on what Celtic wears the shoes that belong with Lucky the Leprechaun's pot of gold.

Not since the ruby red slippers of Oz has there been such an honor. We wonder how much magic there is in green sneaks.

Click twice and score? Celtics must be careful that the wicked witches from Miami and Indiana don't drop a house on the franchise.

Whether the green sneaks are simply an honor, a psychological weapon, or merely a color code easier to see flash on the floor as players dribble up and down, we are not yet sure. The Celtics aren't talking.

Green eggs and green shoes with ham on the side, Dr. Seuss knew an acquired taste when he saw it.

You could do worse than learn that one man wearing green sneakers makes all the difference.

The yoke of scoring may be on the feet of the man in the Celtics colored footwear. You cannot walk on eggshells if you are the Celtic player in the green sneaks.

Celtics Make An Offer Sixers Cannot Refuse

As the Mob members said in *The Godfather,* it may be time for one team to hit the mattresses.

Yes, that smell is actually the Celtic version of Clemenza making meatballs for the gang as they wait to go to war. Mrs. Ray Allen would not approve of this culinary approach for getting ready.

Doc Rivers is now giving Rajon Rondo some good advice right out of the movie: "Take the cannolis, and leave the gun."

Nothing could be worse for the Sixers than waking up for Game 3 and finding a horse's head under the sheets. As Rondo said after the game, "We wanted to send a message."

Yes, a horse's head in bed with you is a message. More likely, the Sixers feel like they are now the other end of the horse.

If you see Brando Rondo running up and down the floor with cotton balls in his cheeks, do not be alarmed. He is waiting for his big closeup.

Despite his arm being in a sling, Sonny Avery wants to take out the crooked Philly cop by shooting threes.

The man pulling the strings on the Big Three is clearly the Celtics' Godfather. If Brando Rondo doesn't given Ray Allen the ball, it could be that Ray has not kissed the hand of the Godfather and paid his respects frequently enough. No, Ray is not a Fredo.

Every godfather must have an enforcer. In this case, it is bellicose KG whose demeanor smacks of killer instinct. He may be asked by the Godfather to do the dirty work, as befits his role.

Every godfather must have a *consigliore*, or mouthpiece, and Paul Pierce will have to do more than his usual taunting and running off at the mouth.

Brando Rondo is still planning a big finish when he will put all his enemies to rest in the Finals. Right now he is just warming up before he takes on the other mob families in Miami and Los Angeles. And, we don't mean those guys with the videocameras.

Zombieland: Icabod Rondo Faces the Walking Dead

In old fashioned Freudian terms, the Boston Celtics are a bunch of masochists. They love to inflict pain on themselves—and the collateral target: their fans are incidental victims.

Wasn't it Oscar Wilde who reminded us that every man kills the thing he loves? The Celtics killed another victory in Game 4.

A coward does it with a word, and a brave man does it with a sword. In this case, the Celtics killed victory without a word to the wise.

The 's' word in the fourth playoff game of the series was "sado-masochistic." The Walking Dead were scary to behold, resisting the final solution and chasing the Celtics all the way back to Boston.

No team can serve two masters (defense and offense), and do justice to both. The Celtics fired their big guns, but the zombies kept coming.

Rondo and the Celtics have just regenerated another zombie team that is now running amok in the playoffs.

Zombies from Philly dashed about the court like headless creatures chasing Ichabod Crane.

We kept waiting for each Sixer to throw his pumpkin head at Rajon Rondo to watch the point guard scramble in six directions.

Avery Bradley looked like a pinball bouncing off the Phillly Sixers. Once bitten, his shoulder seemed ready to fall off.

As in a typical George Romero movie, the game started out with Celtics shooting zombies in a variety of ways, taking a lead and knocking over the Walking Dead with aplomb and amusement.

When the task became tiresome, the zombies knew they had worn down the Celtics. It was a matter of time before the flesh-chompers overran the arrogant Celtics and took a deadly bite out of the heart of the Celtics.

The Green team will soon see daylight again in Boston, but the night will again follow unless they can learn how to play against zombies.

A Big Hand for the Celtics? or The Big Sleep?

Have the Boston Celtics really played "rope a dope" with the Philadelphia 76ers?

Or is it the other way around?

Shall the apparently shell-shocked and demoralized Philly team suddenly surge upward like a tsunami hidden in the ocean until it reaches the Boston shoreline?

These questions should be answered in Game 4 that could tell whether the team that could not win big games on the road has changed its proverbial stripes.

The Celtics never make anything easy, and the Easy Button seems to be stapled to Rajon Rondo's mouth guard. He wore the green sneakers for the big Game 3 victory and went sweat band-less when it came to headwear.

We presume Rondo may be mercurial, but he will be dressed exactly the same for Game 4.

The sense of urgency this postseason transcends all the other years.

Kevin Garnett, Paul Pierce, and Ray Allen, may be familiar with the famous Boston story about the aging political boss who chooses to run one more time for the Big Enchilada. Yes, it was called *The Last Hurrah!*

The Big Three may be facing their own *Big Chill* as well. That was a movie about young people realizing mortality can rear its ugly head at any time. People in the Big Three's generation are being retired summarily all over the NBA.

Right now the fear is that this year's playoffs will turn into *Pee Wee's Big Top* under the Big Top of Shorty Rondo.

Celtics fans just want to avoid the *Big Sleep* for as long as possible, which may follow the *Big Heat* series anyhow.

In the meantime, the *Big Kahuna* remains Banner #18.

Brandon Bass: Neither Fish Nor Foul

Rajon Rondo went Bass fishing in Game 5.

And, he caught a whopper.

For those who had been hoping and expecting a game to be won by those who are not necessarily going to the Hall of Fame, Brandon Bass provided the answer.

Many times over the past few games, the Boston Celtics, favored by most, seemed to look more rumpled than Mark Zuckerberg's wedding suit.

Brandon Bass suddenly showed up in his Sunday-Go-To-Meeting Outfit and sent the Sixers on a fishing expedition.

In a playoff game of his career, the man who exchanged teams with Big Baby Davis during the off-season became the star of the day.

His point total was on the order of a machine, outscoring the entire Sixer team in the third quarter: 18 to 16. His overall total reached 27 points.

Bass is a temperate species, unlike Big Baby fish whose crying jags often sent Kevin Garnett into a state of irritation. This Bass is not the large mouth variety we found in Mr. Davis.

Rondo, an aficionado of music, prefers harmony and rhythmic support. If ever he needed it to round out his continuing-to-escalate number of assists, he found the best music in the Bass player.

Mr. Bass is the fifth chord on the Celtics starting lineup, and now his music has reached a crescendo. It could not have come a moment too soon. The coda is on the horizon, and Bass may be needed one more time in Philadelphia to show up the 76er trombones.

All You Need is Garnett and Rondo

Kevin Garnett loves Boston fans.

He stands in the middle of the court and like a maestro he waves his hands to orchestrate the sounds of the crowd.

He is John Williams with his baton before the Boston Pops. Last season it was Shaquille O'Neal who went to the Pops and conducted the orchestra for several holiday tunes.

Garnett does his conducting only at the Garden. After the victory in playoff Game 5, he waxed eloquent about the Celtic fan base. He seemed to be presenting the theme from "Jaws" to the basketball audience.

If he had hummed the tune, the fans of Philly would have felt teeth biting into their hindquarters.

Garnett indicated that the home noise assisted him and the team come up big in the third period—and conversely seemed to suck the air out of the Sixers.

KG, an astute analyst, noted there are two kinds of fans: the bad kind is a "fair weather fan" that seem to populate arenas from Philadelphia to Atlanta to Miami and beyond.

"It's not even close," reiterated Kevin. Alerted this could be inflammatory to the fans during the next visit to Philly, Garnett scoffed, "Take it how you want."

The ever-slippery Garnett may have been diabolical yet again. He knows how much he feeds off the anger and bile of the opposing fans. They will call him old and dirty, which are names that spur Kevin and put him into the heat mode.

This was more calculated than the *Dark Knight Rising*.

If there is a Robin to the truer Batman in the league, it is Robin Rondo who works so well with Garnett and is attuned to KG's sly and dry wit. They are Ying and Yang on and off court.

When they do press conferences together, Rondo has to glance away and stifle a smile when Garnett throws a look his way.

We'd love to hear Rondo singing: "I've Got You Under My Skin," on his new CD. He'd be thinking of Garnett for sure.

The only way for Philly fans to neutralize Garnett and Rondo is to politely doff their caps and offer a smattering of applause.

Missing in Action and Lost at Sea?

Apparently Boston Celtics' star point guard Rajon Rondo had been replaced in Game 6 by one of the Pod People.

Yes, it appears those unreliable body snatchers showed up to invade the Boston team's seminal head case.

One teammate on the Celtics noticed that a mysterious pretender usurped Rajon Rondo. Captain Paul Pierce recognized the blank stare and unemotional response to pain—and he knew what he must do.

Several times on the bench, The Truth Pierce gave Rondo what could kindly be called a love tap or dope slap on the back of the head.

If Moe had hit Curly this hard, there'd have been only two Stooges.

Paul Pierce hasn't slapped anyone this hard since he defended himself against a knife-wielding assailant in a Boston nightclub in 2000.

Next game Rajon may ask to switch seats with anyone a couple of seats away from Paul. Rondo may have to sit on the opposing team bench because his older brother Paul has long arms and will find the back of his head at some point.

Team trainers did test Rondo for a concussion after his noggin was knocked around. They could hear the marbles rolling around like a pinball machine.

Theories about Rondo's blank stare and absent-minded drooling centered around missing his nap again or having cross words on the phone with Kendrick Perkins earlier in the day.

A few more cynical fans insisted that he had forgotten to take his meds before the game.

Those fans "in the know" realized that Rajon was still upset from seeing his role model Sherlock Holmes die in the final episode of the season on PBS's hit Sunday show.

Elementary Deduction and Smart Play, Sherlock Rondo!

We recently compared Rajon Rondo to Sherlock Holmes, and we were met with a hail of gunfire from Moriarty's forces.

Lest we be accused of making a hasty deduction, let us count the ways.

Doc Rivers more often than not plays the role of Chief Inspector Lestrade whose play calling is clueless, but finds the key man in the field (Sherlock Rondo) constantly discovers the real clues.

Alas, in this version of Holmes, it is the faithful companion, Dr. Watson Perkins who went over Reichenbach Falls without a barrel. It has left Rondo bereft that his amanuensis has gone on to a better playoff team.

Everyone knows that Rondo is smarter than any other player on the court. He sees all and knows all the plays before they happen. One tiny detail reveals to him the scheme of the opposing coach.

Rondo, like Sherlock, has poor social skills and could not be bothered with Facebookian niceties. He will tweet now and then when the mood strikes him. He will unfriend you in a flash.

Sherlock, on occasion, would wear a deerstalker cap, and sometimes Rondo will wear a headband.

Holmes lamented his talents were constantly being used in mundane and boring cases, and Rondo surely would agree that most games are not primetime affairs where he can shine.

Sherlock always listened for the dog that didn't bark in the night, and Rajon listens for KG who never barks in the paint.

Holmes always found irritation with his older brother Mycroft, and Rondo always finds himself put on the spot by his older brother Paul Pierce.

Sherlock surrounded himself with minor players who did his bidding, known as the Baker Street Irregulars. Rondo has a bench of players known as the Causeway Street Irregulars.

Holmes had a housekeeper named Mrs. Hudson who picked up after all his messes, and Rondo has the Boston media.

Rondo Foreshadows Another Playoff Victory

For fans looking for the augurs of victory for the Boston Celtics in their big Game 7 against the Sixers, they had to look only as far as Rajon Rondo.

As he made his way to the clubhouse at the TD Garden, strolling in alone off the street as he often does on a big day, he looked as somber as ever.

Significantly, he was dressed to the Nines, which so happens to be his number.

His street clothes, often a source of controversy as he has to rival the *Fashionista* of Miami Dwyane Wade, were without doubt utilitarian and about as deadly as a Mayan high priest about to cut the heart out of his opponent on the altar of Game 7.

D-Wade wears shocking pink to the game, and Rondo wears your basic black and green to the game.

Yes, hard as it was to believe, Rondo was wearing a green-checkered shirt with solid green collar and black sleeves as he came down Causeway Street. The last time we saw an outfit this audacious it was being worn by Pinky Lee.

Had Rondo stolen his outfit from a dead leprechaun? Well, not stolen perhaps. We couldn't tell if he had on the green emerald slippers with the curl to the toe.

He wore everything shamrock colors--except Lucky the Leprechaun's green derby.

This example of Celtics lore proved that now, more than ever, Rondo would bleed green. This was the prognostication and omen that a legendary member of the Celts was in the house.

As statements go, this one seemed to hold promise of a pot of gold at the end of regulation time.

No one else would dare to usurp the costume of the Celtic mascot as his everyday ware, but the inimitable Rondo was unfazed.

In an unusual turn of events, Rondo appeared to sweat during most of the game, especially when the score was closer than a Hammam steam-room where triple doubles are as hot as it gets.

39 Steps Begins with One Single Step

Can the Celtics step it up for a series against LeBron and Pink-Wade?

We'd say they are facing a step down. If they don't watch that first step, they may end up face down.

If you think the Celtics have a chance to go stepping out with the Heat, you may be taking a long walk off a short pier.

If Celtics fans are looking forward to the Miami Heat game, they may not see the sun's corona from the penumbra. It looks like a step in the wrong direction.

If we start to see Rajon Rondo called for steps during the Miami games, you know the Celtics are one step beyond.

Boston has taken it one step at a time, and still they are tripping over their own two left feet.

It's hard to do a two-step when you have bone spurs in your heels; just ask Ray Allen. When the tough step lively, the lively Celtics are out of step.

So far the Celtics have not taken a step behind the 3-point line with any kind of consistent success. They have become the ugly stepchildren of Celtics history.

There are thirteen steps up to the gallows, and the Celtics may play 13 games before they face the noose that the Miami Heat want to put around their proverbial neck.

We are stepping around the big mess in the middle of the paint for Miami because stepping in it may have a permanent effect on our sneakers.

If Doc Rivers has a plan laid out in Alfred Hitchcock's style of 39 steps, we think it is high time he took the first step to show us.

We are ready for the first step of our long journey through Miami and to the Finals, despite having flat feet.

Boston Sports Fans Name Their Poison

Has Brandon Lloyd of the New England Patriots met his counterpart named Rajon Rondo of the Boston Celtics?

We suspect they will hook up before the NFL season begins when Rondo makes an obligatory appearance at the Patriot training camp sometime in July.

The two birds of a feather join a grand number of odd birds, like Jacoby Ellsbury of the Red Sox and Brad Marchand of the Bruins.

Each of these players has garnered the adjective/cliché, which needs to be retired as it can no longer be used for anyone else.

For example, there can be no mention of Rajon Rondo without noting that he is mercurial. Indeed, many stories cannot go more than a few lines without dubbing the mercurial Rondo as part of his character.

Jacoby Ellsbury, also with a well-earned reputation for singularity, has faced the daunting label of being fragile. Owing to his propensity toward injured ribs, shoulders, and hangnails, Jacoby has taken on the mantle of J.D. Drew—but made it his own as he is mostly fragile. As in: "The fragile Ellsbury resumed rehab."

Brad Marchand has hip-checked more Boston media than just about anyone outside of Josh Beckett. If there is a hyphenated term applied to his daily regimen, it is likely "party-animal." Yes, Brad Marchand never met a night on the town he didn't love.

Now Boston's journalist brigade has met Brandon Lloyd, the new darling of Josh Daniels's offense. Taking none, Brandon Lloyd has a history that blossomed as an adjective label within days of coming to Boston. Yes, he is "troubled." For years, the troubled Lloyd has gone from team to team, finally hoping for a home for troubled players in New England.

Whether Brandon remains "troubled," or Rondo cannot escape his "mercurial" nature, or that Jacoby will always be "fragile," and Brad always a "party-animal," we know that you can count on the right modifier to baptize your favorite athlete in every story.

Boston Celtics: Groundhogs and Underdogs

In *Groundhog Day,* as Bill Murray learned in the classic film, every day you face the same problem.

That vile little rodent may be tormenting the Boston Celtics too. Only now he plays for the Miami Heat.

Nowadays every morning they awake, the Celtics find themselves shutting off the alarm clock and finding out they are the underdogs, not groundhogs.

The Celtics meet the same people every day who ask them the same mundane questions *ad nauseum*. Yes, we mean you, Members of the Media.

Every day we hear that the Celtics are too old and too beaten up.

If going to Miami with predictions of a sweep dancing in their heads seems familiar to you, it's because the Celtics have faced this daunting task more than once.

The Celtics awake each morning to the same nagging injuries of bone spurs, sprained knees, sore feet, and dislocated elbows about to rear their ugly head.

If it seems like a bad dream that will pass, the Celtics must remember that tomorrow will also be today. Every day is Groundhog Day for the Celtics against Miami Heat.

Bettors and aficionados of the NBA will pick the Celtics to be losers again. They will be a day older and will not be getting any younger. The best they can hope for is a holding pattern.

There is always a chance the groundhog Heat will see their shadows and run back into the hole where they usually hibernate.

In the face of all fairy tale endings, we hereby warn the Celtics to be careful what you wish for. That'll be the day indeed.

The dream matchup of facing the dastardly D-Wade and Lebron, media darlings of money shakers and bum kissers, is upon us again and again, like we have a stuck rewind button on the remote.

Yes, LeBron and D-Wade, the remnants of a wannabe Big Three, are preparing the electric chair for their guests. That never changes.

Curmudgeons across the world are uniting against the overly saccharine, undeserving, overblown Miami Heat that are more bombastic than any hurricane in Florida.

Two Head Cases for Dr. Freud and Dr. Jung

Many media mavens have described LeBron as a man on a mission: to prove his mother is not a problem. Along the way to pick up his championship ring, he may have more dust-ups than Dorothy faced on the way to Oz.

NBA fans in the North have described Rajon Rondo as a man on a mission: to prove that he is the key to the success of three future Hall of Famers. He lives in Munchkinland and resents those talking trees.

We don't like to characterize Gloria James as the Wicked Witch, but KG may want to drop a Celtic house on LeBron's house of cards.

Comparing the Miami Big Three to the Oz Big Three, we have a better idea of what the Celtics face: a cowardly lion named LeBron, a Tin Woodsman named Dwyane, and a Scarecrow named Bosh.

The Celtic secret weapon is a little yapping dog named Toto Rondo. He is the spy in the house of the NBA. We've seen him repeatedly listen in on opposing team huddles.

The plain fact is that Heat and Celtics have within their roster the key to success and the same key also opens the door to failure.

Yes, Rondo and James are swords that cut two ways.

You can praise them when they accomplish things like they have arrived on the Chariots of the Gods, but they can also look like they are driving a Tin Lizzie stuck in a pothole.

Rondo and LeBron may be a modern equivalent of David and Goliath, but basketball *cognoscenti* realize Alfred Hitchcock might have cast either one as Norman Bates in *Psycho*.

No doubt, Drs. Sigmund Freud and Carl Jung would have battled over the root cause of Rondo/LeBron Syndrome.

If Rondo Wants Work in Post-Season…Thanatopsis Calls

After watching Rajon Rondo play the unemotional machine in playoff Game 2 with Miami, a few media moguls have wondered what kind of laconic personality lies beneath the surface of the Celtics star point guard.

If Rondo needs something to keep him occupied in the post-season after playing thrill-a-minute basketball, he could find his dour personality is suited to a few interesting jobs.

Based on his cold-blooded demeanor, some fans think he could become the new Orkin bug exterminator. We can see him standing on the front lawn, forcing those cockroaches to drive away in haste.

Sang-froid is also a characteristic that would keep Rondo busy if he chose to be a hired assassin. He shows all the aplomb of Clint Eastwood walking into a corrupt Western town and simply wiping out the bad guys one shot at a time.

We see Rondo driving a speedboat or a race-car, breaking new records. Stepping out of the vehicle after smashing the latest barrier, he would look like he just came from a massage parlor.

A few may say that Rondo ought to be the Greeter at your local funeral parlor, welcoming all those who wish to view the beloved before he is sent off to the crematorium.

If ever there is a need for someone to administer a lethal injection, Rondo could show up at Texas prisons and send the convicted to the next level of his game.

In terms of sports, Rondo is probably a match up for driving a dog sled at the Iditarod race in Alaska. He may not even need the dogs.

We still think Rondo's unique talents would be perfect as an efficiency expert that comes into a new company and summarily fires everyone.

If you need someone to pry open that oyster and take the pearl, you should call Rajon Rondo.

Who's the Queen of the Boston Celtics?

When Ray Allen speaks, the world listens. After the recent playoff game, he said the series between Miami and Boston was like a game of chess.

Ray then went one move beyond. He said the real strategy hinged on the Queen of each team. Ray said, "They took our queen, and we took theirs."

Good heavens, this came from our Knight in Shining Armor.

We know that LeBron James is some kind of basketball royalty, but we thought he was merely a pretender to the throne. Now we learn that his kingship may be in Queensland.

More appalling by Ray was his amusing dig at his own teammate and closest relation outside the brotherhood.

He referred to Paul Pierce as a queen, not as his twin Knight of the three-pointer.

In all our days, we thought of Paul as a randy bishop, or a bit of a Rook in his younger days. Now we learn that he is the queen of queens.

Perhaps Ray merely misspoke and used his metaphors in a loose fashion, as we all know that Rondo is the Queen of the Celts, and Paul is the Queen Mother.

In terms of fashion, Rondo surely holds court as the one in the more flouncy outfits, as befitting Marie Antoinette of the Guards.

We suppose this makes Kevin Garnett the centerpiece or King of the squares. He certainly knows how to plop himself into the sweet spot and stay there.

Basketball is a game of chess moves, but we feel like we have been checkmated by Ray Allen in the humor department.

Rondo Joins the Next Generation of Star Trek

When Rajon Rondo showed up at Game 4 of Miami and Boston wearing one of the *Star Trek* jerseys, we knew it was time to beam him up.

No, Rondo was not wearing Captain Kirk's jersey. That would be totally inappropriate. If he should wear anyone's jersey, it would belong to Mr. Spock. We do not mean Zachary Quinto, but the original brainiac of the team, Leonard Nimoy.

Of course, true aficionados of *Star Trek* would immediately recognize that Rondo had actually dipped into the 1980s version of *Star Trek: the Next Generation*. Calling Mr. Blackwell! Fans from Miami would have pegged Rondo as a Romulan, but he is clearly Vulcan.

His two-tone jersey, with the different color across the shoulder was the height of the fashion for Captain Picard, but we realized that Rondo was actually in the uniform of Geordie (played by Levar Burton).

As we recall, Geordie was blind and wore a special kind of dark glasses, quite similar to the sort the NBA banned Rondo from wearing on the court.

Rondo definitely has the shoulders for an outfit that highlights the sway of his gait. He may have the demeanor of Wil Wheaton, but he comes across with a dash of Sulu.

We are not sure how significant Rondo's return to the previous generation of *Star Trek* may be. It would seem he has just beamed down with a supply of Dilithium Crystals to help the Celtics shoot into warp drive during Game 4.

Then again, Hollywood is holding auditions for the new movie sequel with Chris Pine and Zachary Quinto. Rondo is ahead of the curve as always.

Boston Mayor Malaprop Mouths Off at the Celtics

Boston's Mayor Thomas Mumbles Menino has fractured the Boston sports scene yet again with his unique brand of enunciating for world of championship athletes. Mrs. Malaprop had nothing on Mayor Mumbles Mintendo.

A big fan of winning teams and victor of many a wager with rival team mayors, Mumbles Manolito has opened the oral gap again and stuck in a silver foot.

During Super Bowl week he waxed eloquent on the stars of the New England Patriots, citing the heroic and legendary qualities of the biggest stars: West Weckler and Ron Grabowski.

Searching high and low upon the Patriot roster, we did find Weckler and Grabowski playing under assumed names of Wes Welker or Rob Gronkowski.

Mayor Mumbles Manoverboardo has now come to praise the Boston Celtics as they return home to face the Heat. In Boston tenement apartments, you know how to control the heat: you rap three times on the radiator. He rapped hard three times to knock the Heat out of the pipes.

Always good for a bite of sound, Tom Menatworko stopped to chat with the media again today and singled out the hard work and impressive qualities of his favorite Celtic players, "KJ and Hondo."

Mumbles knows full well that KJ means a Karaoke Joe and Hondo is one of the all-time great Celtics. Like the modern day Rajon Rondo, John 'Hondo' Havlicek could run for forty minutes in a game and not sweat. KG or Kevin Garnett's name has a certain ring to it.

Havlicek once famously stole the ball, according to Johnny Most, and Mayor Mensmencho could have a brainlock that causes him to see Hondo where he means Rondo.

If pressed, we are sure Mayor Mumbles will gladly inform us that he has admired KJ since the days when he sang with that Sunshine Band out of Miami.

Boston has been blessed with a roster domain of sport names that are eminently unforgettable. KP and Fondu are just a few.

Celtics Offer Dickens of a Run

What noble words did Rondo say at the postgame press conference? We did not hear, "It is a far, far better thing that I do, than I have ever done; it is a far far better rest that I go to than I have ever known."

Sydney Carton was a version of Rajon Rondo. He was destined to appear on the proverbial milk carton after the Miami Heat and Celtics battled during Game 7.

If you think it's the best of times, you live in Miami. If you think it's the worst of times, you live in Boston. If you think the games were fixed, you may be living in cynicism.

It was a far, far better journey to get this far with three series of seven games. The Big Three go to a far far better rest than they have ever known. It was the season Byrds sing about, Ecclesiastes.

Charles Dickens always knew the right moment to bless us every one, and the right time to curse with "Bah, humbug."

Start singing *A Christmas Carol* because the Celtics are deader than a doornail this season.

It looks like Christmas came early for one team, and like *Oliver Twist,* fans of the other team are asking for "More, sir, please."

The Celtics ended up wishing *David Copperfield* put a little magic on their team. Whether the Celtics turn out to be the heroes of the game has been answered with a thud.

If the TD Garden starts to look like *Bleak House* this summer, it is only because the Celtics' *Great Expectations* and Big Three have been blown to the four winds.

Hard Times have fallen on a once proud championship franchise, or at least till the *Cliff Notes* version of the Big Three comes to the rescue with a couple of young big men.

Our Mutual Friend Rajon Rondo and *Little Dorrit* Avery Bradley agree that the Celtics tale ends up a bit like the *Mystery of Edwin Drood*—an unfinished epic.

Dickens always made his stories run a little longer than you would have liked, but not long enough this time.

Rondo Becomes the Real Deal: a Superstar!

The amazing Rajon Rondo of the Boston Celtics turned the corner on legacy in a losing effort in Game 2 of the Heat-Celtics playoff matchup.

Rondo put on his whirling dervish personality and spun faster and faster, like he was the ballerina in *The Red Shoes*.

Playing every minute of an overtime game, he transfixed the television audience and naysayers by remaining on court without break for 53 minutes, scoring 44 points.

Rondo detractors will probably point out that he fell short of a triple/double and did not win the game singlehandedly. A few may even say Wilt Chamberlain did it better.

On a day when the unlikely became the shocking and events turned surprising, Rondo stood out over the likes of Justin Bieber and Tom Brady.

Slim and slight, no hot-tempered tough guy Justin Bieber (reportedly sought by police) assaulted an annoying member of the Paparazzi. Slight and babyish, Justin should bask in his new reputation.

Mild-mannered and polite Tom Brady (appearing in an Under Armour commercial) assaulted an annoying store clerk. The irritating salesman insisted Brady had a Boston accent.

Tom Brady's latest foray into TV acting may win him a gig on *True Blood* where everyone has a funny accent. Tom plays himself as a Bostonian in denial.

These three made the world better for a few moments to the delight of their fans. Who knew?

Nothing could be better for the world than to see someone trying to tip over windmills with a lance from their arsenal.

Don Quioxte gave us an impossible dream—but only Rondo turned it into the stuff of real life drama. Rondo dismissed the feat as "irrelevant" if you lose the game.

Though Rondo may deny it, he moved on to the next level in sports history with his performance, something to be remembered as a man giving the full measure in the face of adversity.

To be willing to give when there's no more in the tank, Rondo can one day rest with the certain knowledge that he reached for the sobriquet of "Superstar" on this night—and he made it.

AND AT LAST...

Celtics Big Three: The Next Generation

Star Trek simply retooled its cast and went back into space. So may it be for the Boston Celtics. These are the voyages of the creaky starship Celtics. Its mission is to reconstitute and boldly go forth.

What's that mean for the Celtics?

Ray Allen doesn't want to play with Rondo after this season.

Kevin Garnett does want to play with his little Shorty Rondo. The Skipper and Gilligan need each other.

Paul Pierce actually likes Rondo.

Brandon Bass loves playing with Rondo.

Avery Bradley has met a soul mate in Rondo. There are still restaurants on the road where they have not yet eaten together.

We can't make it any simpler. The rest of that team goes where the wind of Fate takes them, or in this case where Danny Ainge sends them.

Bull and former Celtic and constant Rondo admirer Brian Scalabrine may return to Boston on the broadcast desk.

We can expect Jeff Green and Chris Wilcox will return for a shot at immortality under the wing of Rajon Rondo. Greg Stiemsma seems to be a Rondo guy.

After that, Danny Ainge can scour the ranks of NBA players who could take a chance on Boston. The list may be smaller than Bostonians would think—shocked, shocked, shocked to learn NBA stars aren't enamored of the local baked beans.

Of course, Doc Rivers will still be here, and he may be playing *Father Knows Best* with his own son, Austin.

The wild card remains the inscrutable Dwight Howard. No one will want him—except Rondo.

These are the continuing voyages of the Starship Celtics.

Books about sports by William Russo:
GREAT SPORTS STORIES: THE LEGENDARY FILMS
SEX, DRUGS, SPORTS, & WHIMSY
SEX, DRUGS, SPORTS & WHIMSY, Volume 2
RAJON RONDO: SUPERSTAR!
DEATH, TAXES & SPORTS WHIMSY
RED SOX 2011: A WHIMSICAL AUTOPSY
NEW ENGLAND PATRIOT WHIMSY
TEBOW VERSUS GRONK
LIES, STATISTICS & SPORTS WHIMSY
TALES OF THE NBA: ARROGANCE, IDIOCY & WHIMSY

Books in the Mal Tempo Series
MAL TEMPO
MAL TEMPO & FRIENDS
WHEN BILLY THE KID MET BEN HUR…
NECROSERV
DIARY OF MAL TEMPO
PICNIC WITH MELVILLE & HAWTHORNE
A WALK WITH MAL TEMPO (film)
Books co-authored by William Russo and Jan Merlin:
THE PAID COMPANION OF John Wilkes Booth
TROUBLES IN A GOLDEN EYE
MGM MAKES BOYS TOWN
HANGING WITH BILLY BUDD
FRANKIE THOMAS: THE ETERNAL CADET
Books by William Russo:
AUDIE MURPHY IN VIETNAM
RIDING JAMES KIRKWOOD'S PONY
DUMB-FOUNDED: THE STORY OF THE AMERICAN LANGUAGE
BOOTH AND OSWALD
THE NEXT JAMES DEAN

All books are available in print and in e-book format from Kindle, Nook, Smashwords and Google Books.

Dr. William Russo writes books for all occasions. The former college professor slums as a Hollywood tabloid sensation-seeking columnist. Nowadays he remains in seclusion. He can be reached on Facebook at Long Time Ago Books or on Twitter @ossurworld. Many—but not all--of the essays included here have already appeared in other books and on websites like The Spoof and MTR Media.

18706857R00110

Made in the USA
Lexington, KY
19 November 2012